CW00797363

YAFFA GOLAN PUBLISHING
Hanegev 4 TEL-AVIV 66186
I S R A E L
TEL: 972-3-6870088   FAX: 972-3-6881443

Comments about "Stop the Stress"

"Stop the Stress" and the Silva Method changed my way of thinking and helped me in managing my personal life. As a business woman handling great responsabilities and facing day-to-day decisive questions for which I must find the answer, I am subject to inordinate amounts of stress. *"Stop the Stress"* and its relaxation method taught me how to manage with this daily stress. It also helped me to handle personal situations in a better and more positive way, and I even transmitted this new way of thinking to my family members. "Everyone should read *"Stop the Stress"* in order to improve his or her way of life."
> Yaffa Golan
> President of a group of six companies, including
> Diet Deal Ltd.
> Israel

"I read your book, *"Stop the Stress"* with great interest. The book sheds light on our tense and tumultuous lives. The style is clear and lucid, even for a person who has no previous knowledge of the Silva Method.
For those who have participated in the course, the contents of the book are even more helpful. The text succinctly summarizes the central points of the Silva Method, a proven tool for reduction in tension and pressure. *"Stop the Stress"* is essential reading for anyone interested in living a more relaxed, less stressful life.
Thank you, Tania and Rafi for this clear and easily-understood guide for any reader.
The Silva Method, like your book, always awakens in me a continual sense of wonder, influencing my life and improving my day to day living. Many thanks,"
> Judge (emeritus) Haim Eilat
> Israel

"Reading *"Stop the Stress"* is itself a vacation from stress. Following the simple relaxation procedures is even more of a relief from every day complexities. This book is a must for anybody having to cope with today's problems – a stress-buster and a life-extender."

Robert B. Stone Ph.D.
Author and co-author of 81 published books in 15 languages
USA

"The authors Liberman give us coaching in mental housecleaning to help us clean up our act, to even change unwanted, damaging habits like addictions to negative thinking and speaking, smoking and overeating. They even share techniques for improving our sexual relationships, improving creativity, and getting helpful information from our subconscious mind...You will enjoy and profit from this book!"

Harry McKnight Ph.D.
USA

"Stop the Stress," the latest book on the renowned Silva Method, is also one of the best. Graphics are designed to simplify the method and the relaxation techniques lead you to a stress-free life in a happy, and more productive work environment. I highly recommend it."

Burt Goldman
Author of *"Better and Better"* and *"The Silva Mind Control Method of Mental Dynamics"*
USA

"This book sums up many sources of thought and wisdom that have accrued through the years. For someone who is familiar with most of these concepts, the book serves as a good refresher course. It also provides a convenient CD for applying and implementing what one already knows. For someone for whom the concepts are new, the book provides a stimulating and convenient way to acquire this practical and important knowledge. I began to use the Method again, and I greatly enjoy the feeling of control and the ability to influence my mind and daily activity."

  Prof. Yehiel Ziv
  Tel-Aviv University
  Israel

"When many years ago I searched for the definition of relaxation in the 1965 edition of the Even-Shoshan dictionary, I could not find the word. This reflects the lack of awareness. Perhaps the urgency was not as great then it seems to be today. And filling this genuine need is the book by Tania and Rafael Liberman, *"Stop the Stress."* In clear and thoughtful language – almost like a story – the basics of relaxation are described. Various relaxation techniques are presented, as well as a CD – it is attractive and valuable for everyone."

  Hadassah Tal Ph.D.
  Israel

"Readers who are interested in coping with tension will find several solutions to their problems in this the book and CD. It is a stimulus for deepening the reader's understanding and ability to use the Silva Method."

  Yigal Harpaz, Ph.D.
  Israel

Three testimonies from an Arab family

"I had no prior knowledge of the Silva Method, had no idea what it was about. I contacted Mr. Moshe Liberman who gave me an explanation that intrigued me, so I bought two books on the Silva Method. One of them was *"Stop the Stress."* This book was very different. I did the exercises together with my wife and three children. Since then, my wife has done the 12-minute pause exercise every day after work and all the pressure of her work day dissipates and she can get very relaxed and calm. I also recommended the book to a friend of mine who started doing the relaxation exercises, and he was able to give up smoking, something he had never been able to do!"

      Nadim Daoud
      Rama Village, Upper Galilee, Israel

"When my husband brought the book *"Stop the Stress"* home, I began looking through it. I soon discovered it was no ordinary book, but a book that makes psychology easy to understand and put into practice. As I continued the exercises, I learned to become more and more relaxed. Today I have reached a point where I can spontaneously do some of the techniques at work or afterwards. The exercises relieve the pressure of my work day and help me reach a wonderful state of relaxation."

      Wafa Farag Daoud

"I am 15 years old, a student in the ninth grade. I practiced the techniques in the book *"Stop the Stress"* that reduce tension and introduced the book to several of my classmates. We organized an exercise on the day of an important math exam and were really surprised when we sat down to take the exam, calm and relaxed. Our grades were much better than we could have hoped for!"

      Elias Rama Daoud

"By only investing a short amount of time the reader can recharge his or her mental and physical batteries to cope with every day problems."

> Tova Trevitz Ph. D.
> Molecular Plant Physiology and Biology
> Weizmann Institute
> Israel

"This book provided me with a new positive outlook on life. I had forgotten what it was like to see the glass half-full instead of half-empty. The relaxation techniques gave me a feeling of serenity and well-being, increased my self-esteem, and gave me more control over household affairs and the children's behavior."

> Esti Rahimi
> Homemaker
> Israel

"I underwent a severe crisis in my life, which was difficult for me to recover from. I was filled with fear and didn't know where to turn. Then I found the book *"Stop the Stress."* I started doing the relaxation exercises, and in a short time, I experienced the beginning of a great change in me. I started to feel how the relaxation techniques were doing wonders for my tension and nerves. For the first time in a long time, I was peace with myself.

"The next stage was finding answers to the problems that plagued me. The CD and the book helped me to think clearly and make the necessary changes. Today I enjoy life and I am more calm and serene."

> Anat Shoher
> Student
> Israel

"Is each one of us aware of the need to carry on an internal dialogue with ourselves? *"Stop the Stress,"* based on the Silva Method, written by Tania and Rafael Liberman, brings each of us to full awareness of this need [...] I tried it, and had an unforgettable experience!"

> Rachel Babad
> Former coordinator of Literature and Language
> State Religious Schools, Israeli Ministry of Education
> and Culture
> Israel

"This book, together with an accompanying CD, deals with reduction of stress and improving memory, concentration and creativity. [...] The proposed daily exercise helps improve the quality of work of managers and workers."

> From the daily "Yediot Aharonot"
> Israel

"Instead of biting your nails and losing your mind, you can exercise your brain and body to be calm exactly when external pressure is on the rise [...]Relaxation helps concentration and lowers cholesterol."

> From the daily "Ma'ariv"
> Israel

"As a person who has been acquainted with the Silva Method for many years and has read a great deal of literature on the subject and followed the progression of public awareness of the Silva Method in Israel, I can vouch for the effectiveness and wide scope of the book *"Stop the Stress,"* which brings to light the many aspects of relaxation technique.

"The book is written in a clear, readable style, suitable for everyone.

Together with the instructional CD which helps to reduce stress, this is the best gift one can give a busy person in these hectic, modern times."

Dalia Mazori

Journalist

Israel

STOP THE STRESS

FOR PERSONAL GROWTH

STOP THE STRESS

FOR PERSONAL GROWTH

Instructional CD Included

12 MINUTE pause

TANIA LIBERMAN   RAFAEL LIBERMAN

in collaboration with

JOSE SILVA

Published by Liber Self-Help Books

Publisher's Note

"Stop the Stress" is based on the knowledge and personal experience of Tania and Rafael Liberman, using the internationally recognized Silva Method and advanced international academic research in the field of relaxation. This kit is not a substitute for psychological or medical care.

Art Director: Moises Liberman
Translation from the Hebrew: Gila Svirsky
Cover & Graphic Design: Moni Blech, "Procolor"
CD Music: Noam Atlas
CD Narrator: Jerry Hyman
Poetry: Adula
Watercolors: Betty Rubinstein

For information contact: Liber Self-Help Books
P.O.Box: 23811, Tel- Aviv 61237 Israel
E-Mail: Liber_Books@bigfoot.com

Library of Congress Cataloging-in-Publication Data

Tania Liberman - Rafael Liberman
Stop the Stress for personal growth
in collaboration with Jose Silva
1st Liber Self-Help ed. 1999
1. Relaxation 2. Positive thinking 3. Self-esteem
4. Children 5. Pregnancy and childbirth. I.Title.
Includes bibliographical references and index.
Includes CD for self-training relaxation.

ISBN 965-222-915-6

10 9 8 7 6 5 4 3 2 1 hard cover

First Edition

"I congratulate the Liberman
family for writing this very
timely book on stress.
This book will help many
to live a healthier, happier
and longer life."

Jose Silva

American researcher Jose Silva is the founder
of the Silva Method.
The Silva Method course has been taught
in more than one-hundred countries
around the world, since 1966.

Dedicated:

To you, the one and only person
who can change your life
for the better.

Contents

Photographs

Acknowledgments

To **Yaffa Golan** whose moral and financial help made the publication of this book possible.

To **Moises**, **Meira**, **Gabi**, and **Gila Liberman** for their important conceptual and practical contributions.

To **Richard Emilio Oulahan**, who helped us with the new English version of the book.

To **the course graduates** and **our other friend** who read the manuscript and gave us their feedback.

To **Juan Silva**, co-Founder of Silva International Inc. who has warmly supported our efforts throughout the years.

To **Jose Silva**, the Creator of the Silva Method and Founder of Silva International Inc., who provided us with the basis and the inspiration to write this book.

Preface

After many years of teaching the Silva Method in Israel, we are pleased to present a book and an accompanying CD, the *"12-Minute Pause,"* that teaches relaxation and its benefits. Our aim is to provide an efficient tool for learning the fundamental principles of relaxation and practice exercises which will reduce stress and improve daily functioning.

This book provides a theoretical and practical basis for coping with stress. We'll talk about overstress and how it affects us. We'll look at a range of possible reactions and suggest ways to cope effectively with stress. We'll teach you how to use relaxation to improve your health, to sleep better, to overcome fatigue, and to improve your success at work, business, and studies.

We'll look at relaxation as a way to strengthen self-confidence and improve sexual functioning. While relaxed we'll overcome the fear of flying. We'll suggest ways to eliminate undesirable habits such as overeating and smoking, and we'll see how we can use relaxation for creative thinking, increasing self-awareness, and setting and achieving goals.

We'll learn how to think positively and how to instill positive thinking in our children. Women will learn how to use relaxation to facilitate pregnancy and childbirth. The book also includes a personal questionnaire to help you evaluate your progress in learning relaxation.

The book comes with a CD that includes the exercise *"12-Minute Pause,"* a 12-minute exercise to help you learn relaxation in an enjoyable manner. The soothing voice and background music in this short exercise augment the instructions and enhance the conditions for relaxation.

There are subliminal positive messages in the exercise. A subliminal message is a message broadcasted on a frequency that our brain is able to absorb and be influenced by, although we cannot hear it consciously. In a relaxed situation, the positive messages recorded on the CD in a subliminal way are directly absorbed by our brain. Many stimuli, both optical and verbal, are absorbed by the brain when transmitted on a wavelength that the eye and ear cannot assimilate under normal conditions. There are differences of opinion among researchers as to the extent of the effect of subliminal aural stimuli. In any case if you know the messages you will hear ahead of time, you can benefit from their positive influence each time you perform the exercise.

The subliminal messages included on the CD are:

Concentration and memory
1. **My concentration and memory improve daily.**

Learning
2. **I learn easily.**

Attitude
3. **I always see the glass half-full.**

Success
4. **I succeed at everything I do.**

Confidence
5. **I am self confident and project this to others.**

Interpersonal relationships
6. **I am a warm person who gives and receives love.**

Health
7. **My healing mind keeps me healthy.**

8. **I feel better and better every day.**

Driving
9. **I drive confidently, carefully and wisely.**

Relaxation
10. **I practice relaxation and enjoy its benefits.**

You be asking yourself, can something so simple as relaxation have such powerful results? Is it possible to achieve all these benefits through relaxation?

The answer is yes! – Not after one or two sessions, but gradually, through daily practice, like the regular training of an athlete.

The *"12-Minute Pause"* does not disconnect you from your world, but helps you cope with it better, and lets you get in touch with your inner consciousness (previously known as the subconscious), helping you live a more harmonious life.

We wish you pleasant reading and enjoyment of all the many benefits of relaxation.

Tania Liberman
Rafael Liberman

Introduction

How hard it is to make the difficult easy!
Juan Ramon Jimenez

Relaxing is an innate, natural human ability. Cultures of the Far East have recognized and enjoyed its benefits for over 3,000 years. In the western world, it was not until the early 20th century that relaxation was studied in a scientific manner.

Today the benefits of relaxation have been proven through many studies and are no longer just a matter of faith. We will briefly survey the history of relaxation and then look at the special features of the kit "Stop the Stress for Personal Growth" and the exercise, the *"12-Minute Pause."*

In the early part of the 20th century, Dr. Edmond Jacobson studied the relationship between muscular tension and fear. He developed a method of progressive relaxation in which all the muscles of the body are gradually contracted and released.

In the 1920s, Dr. H. H. Shultz developed a method known as autogenic training. With this method, the individual focuses on specific physiological functions usually controlled by the autonomous nervous system (such as heartbeat and body temperature). Simple instructions are repeated – "My right hand is warm" or "My heart is beating more slowly" – in an effort to achieve physical and mental relaxation.

In the 1960s, Dr. Herbert Benson of the Harvard Medical School studied meditation as practiced in Japanese Zen Buddhism and Indian Yoga. Benson found that during relaxation, physiological changes occur that do not take place during sleep, and that these help reduce stress. He called these changes "the relaxation response." Benson's studies were the first scientific investigation of the effects of relaxation.

At the same time, biofeedback devices were developed that provide information that could be viewed on a screen about physical processes of which we are unaware, such as the rate of our heartbeat or mental activity. These devices were developed to help bring these processes under voluntary control (such as slowly reducing the rate of heartbeat). However, most people are able to achieve relaxation without recourse to external devices.

Today there are many methods of relaxation, including the Silva Method, developed by the American researcher Jose Silva, and taught since 1966. The Silva Method uses relaxation as a basis for mental training techniques that focus on problem solving and reaching personal goals.

This kit is based on knowledge and personal experience acquired through the Silva Method, as well as on advanced international research in the field of relaxation.

The kit includes many innovations to help you understand the benefits of relaxation on your own, without the assistence of an outside instructor:

- The book includes techniques and tips on how to better cope with difficult situations.

- The short, 12-minute exercise on the CD will help you make time for yourself in order to learn relaxation.

- During the exercise you will be given tips that help you use your imagination in a practical way so that you can obtain better results.

- The exercise is accompanied by original music that reinforces the verbal message.

- To evaluate your progress, a questionnaire was created that will help you monitor the level of relaxation you reach during each exercise.

The book, together with the CD, comprise a practical and efficient kit to help you learn relaxation on your own.

Some Good Reasons for Learning Relaxation

- To attain a pleasurable feeling of calmness.

- To acquire an anti-stress technique that will help at work or elsewhere.

- To prepare for stressful situations: exams, important meetings, confrontations, etc.

- To calm down after a difficult event (a fright, receiving bad news, etc.).

- To eliminate psychosomatic ailments.

- To prepare for physical or mental exertion: sports, public speaking, and presentations.

- To help evoke creative ideas for artists or anyone who wishes to be more creative at work or in personal relationships.

- To teach children and teenagers how to make relaxation an integral part of their lives for maintaining emotional balance and good health.

1
The Dynamics of Stress

CHAPTER 1

The Dynamics of Stress

Accumulated stress can cause both,
physiological and psychological damage.

Overstress

Linda moves restlessly in her chair, her right foot taps rapidly on
the floor, her entire body is tense. The exam will begin in another
10 minutes.

Rick paces the hallway, his hair unkempt from his running his
fingers through it. From time to time, he puts his ear to the door
and listens. On the other side, his wife Carol is in the process of
giving birth to their son. He is not able to be by her side.

Tom's a bundle of nerves. He's been stuck in traffic for a quarter
of an hour, and hasn't moved ahead more than 50 feet. Of all days,
the day he has an important meeting with his boss, he's going to
be late. He looks at his watch again and again, waiting for the light
to turn green. His entire body is tense, he is hunched over the
steering wheel, his hand on the horn, and ready to let the other
drivers know that the light has changed. Get going already!

Linda, Rick and Tom are in a state of stress. Stress is an inevitable
part of daily life. In its positive form, stress spurs us to take initiative
and carry out our plans. Often, however, we find ourselves in a
situation of too much stress, stress that is not efficient. This is
negative overstress, which can damage our health and be an obstacle
that prevents us from achieving goals we have set for ourselves.

Stress accumulates when we don't meet the demands of our work, our studies, our families (external demands), or when we are unable to carry out the tasks that we undertake (internal demands). Stress-causing factors can be strained relationships, financial problems, illness, separation, the death of a loved one, worry, guilt feelings, anger, frustration, and disappointments.

The more we are subject to such situations, the more stress accumulates. In a state of stress, it's difficult to access the resources to cope with demands and function well.

Some people use tranquilizers or sedatives to obtain temporary relief from stress. The use of such pills, however, can decrease motor skills and cause accidents, careless driving, mistakes at work, and the like. What's more, although taking pills provides an escape from the stress, it's not a good way to deal with it. The method proposed in this book, on the other hand, offers a technique that helps you relieve stress and cope with pressure situations, while using your own natural abilities.

How We Respond

Everyone responds differently to demands and each response brings a certain level of stress. The desirable level is, of course, positive stress that stirs us to action.

To a great extent, personality patterns determine the type of response to a given situation. Two people will react differently in the same circumstances. Take, for example, two mothers whose sons get hurt while playing in the yard. One mother will burst out screaming and not know what to do or how to help her son. The other mother, despite her fears and distress, will calm her son down, apply first aid, and arrange to get him to a nearby hospital. Both women feel stress, but they react differently. The first mother is paralyzed by stress, while the other effectively copes with it.

You can learn how to react more effectively in stressful situations, to solve problems better, and to save yourself from unnecessary suffering. Even when events are not under your control, you can always change your response instead of giving in to helplessness and frustration. The first step in relieving overstress is to become aware of its existence.

The first step, therefore, is to identify overstress.

Identifying Stress

The following questions will help you determine if you're in a state of overstress

- Do you get angry easily?
- Is it hard for you to concentrate on what you're doing?
- Do you lose your patience quickly?
- Do you worry too much?
- Do you often feel your heart pounding?
- Do you have difficulties in breathing?
- Do you often feel depressed?
- Do you tend to be aggressive?
- Is it hard for you to make decisions?
- Do you feel alone?
- Have you lost interest in things you used to care about (work, hobbies, sex, etc.)?
- Do you suffer from fatigue or insomnia?
- Do you use sleeping pills to get to sleep?
- Have you recently been overeating, drinking too much, or smoking?
- Do you use drugs or medication without a doctor's prescription?
- Have you suffered lately from such ailments as migraine, backaches, diarrhea, or skin problems?

If you answered "yes" to several of the questions above, you have accumulated overstress and you should release it. (Of course, it's always wise to consult your physician.)

Damage Caused by Stress

Accumulated stress can cause both physiological and psychological damage.

Physiological Effects of Stress

Early in human history, people had to successfully face many dangers to survive. When primitive man met up with a hungry tiger, his body would get ready to spring into action. The man would become tense and begin to sweat, his muscles would contract, his heart would beat rapidly, his mouth would become dry, his blood would flow to his limbs to help him in the battle, or it would flow to his legs should he choose to flee. Preparation of the body for fight or flight is called the survival response.

Even today, human beings respond as if they were risking survival. The brain produces chemicals that send messages to prepare the body for an act of fight or flight. We might feel fear when confronted with verbal aggression (even though there's no physical danger) or when rejected by someone we love, or when taking an exam, applying for a job, facing an operation, or retiring from a career.

Our body responds the same way as that of the early man. Even though we don't have to grapple with a hungry tiger, today we are struggling with mental tigers that may be no less dangerous than the real thing.

Whenever the brain registers a dangerous situation, several chemicals are produced that prepare the body for a fight or flight response. When a situation is perceived as threatening, the brain goes on alert and activates two physiological pathways:

1. the sympathetic nervous system – the adrenal gland

2. the hypothalamus – the pituitary gland – the adrenal cortex

Hypothalamus - Pituitary gland
Adrenal gland

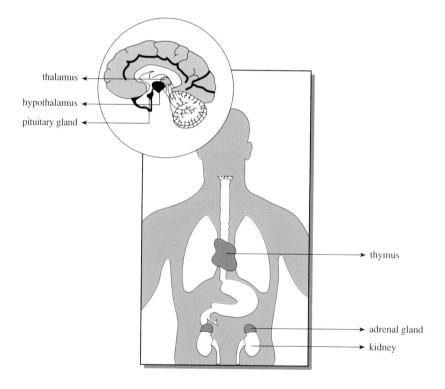

The first pathway stimulates the body to aggressive behavior for coping with a threat or demand, or for fleeing from it. Agitated states of fear (flight) or anger (fight) release certain hormones: adrenaline in a situation of fear and noradrenaline in a situation of anger. These hormones are dispersed throughout the body and bring about:

- Increased blood pressure and heart rate to supply more blood to the muscles and strengthen them for fight or flight.

- Increased blood-sugar levels required for muscle contractions.

- Increased sweating to cool the body in anticipation of exertion.

- Dryness in the mouth from lack of saliva, and other digestive activity following the shutdown of the digestive system to conserve all available energy for the anticipated exertion.

Although following this response the body is ready for action (fight or flight), action is not always the result. For example, a suspicious noise awakens us at night and we're sure there are burglars in the house. After a moment, however, it becomes clear that it was just the cat. Meanwhile, the body has set off a state of alert. Hormones are released quickly, within twenty or thirty seconds, but neutralizing these hormones takes several minutes. Repeated instances in which the body prepares for action that does not occur causes tension to accumulate. For example, there are many situations in which we feel threatened (the boss is angry with us), but we cannot escape, and thus tension accumulates without finding an outlet in physical activity.

Stress also activates the second pathway (hypothalamus – pituitary gland – adrenal cortex). Emotional states of powerlessness or "giving up" stimulate the release of chemicals that enter the bloodstream, whereupon they weaken the immune system and bring about swelling of the joints, rheumatic aches, and constriction of the blood vessels that could precipitate high blood pressure, heart problems, and even stroke.

All the reactions of the autonomous nervous system take place repeatedly during times of real danger (seeing a car about to run you over in the street) or during imaginary dangers (your young son is late getting home and you imagine that something has happened to him).

When situations of stress become frequent, all it takes is a small stimulus to activate a reaction by the autonomous nervous system. We become sensitive to stress, and this sensitivity sometimes brings on problems and ailments.

Ailments Caused by Stress

Blood System	
High blood pressure	Due to constriction of blood vessels and increased adrenalin levels
Stroke	Resulting from high blood pressure
Heart attack	From constriction of the coronary blood vessels, irregular blood supply
Arteriosclerosis	Building of fatty substances in the blood vessels and increased cholesterol
Digestive System	
Constipation, diarrhea, heartburn, vomiting	Contractions of the digestive tract which impair digestion
Ulcer	Increased secretion of gastric and digestive juices

Respiratory System	
Respiratory problems, asthma	Due to narrowed breathing passages in the lungs resulting from increased adrenaline
Muscular System	
Muscle cramps, headaches, rheumatism	Due to secretion of prolactin from the pituitary gland and prolonged contraction of muscles

Psychological Effects of Stress

The adrenaline released in stressful situations often causes anger, which can bring about physical or verbal aggression. The more often this occurs, the more the individual loses control and self-confidence.

When stress builds up, the body is fatigued, the power to concentrate is diminished, and learning abilities are impaired. In order to learn, there must be motivation and power to concentrate. Stress undermines both. First, desire dissipates. The individual is too consumed by worry and personal concerns to truly want to remember what has to be learned. Second, the myriad of thoughts and feelings that arise divert attention away from the material to be learned and further interfere with concentration.

2
The Dynamics of Relaxation

CHAPTER 2

The Dynamics of Relaxation

Some skills are used when you're in touch with the external world, and others when you're in touch with your internal world, in a state of relaxation.

"You're very tense lately and that's not healthy," says Lee to her husband, Robby. "How about trying the relaxation exercise that I do?" "Don't bother me with your relaxation exercises. I sit in my chair, watch the football game on TV, and that calms me down. That's my relaxation."

Perhaps watching television does calm Robby down, but this is not relaxation. Football can distract him from the causes of his stress for a while, but the tension remains in his body. Many people think they can achieve relaxation while watching TV, playing sports, or going on vacation. This is not so. When you are truly in a state of relaxation, many physiological changes take place in the body.

Physiological Effects of Relaxation

Scientifically speaking, relaxation refers to the release and extension of muscles, while tension refers to their contraction and flexion. In a state of relaxation, the following physiological changes can be discerned:

A. Change in brain wave activity
B. Decreased respiration rate
C. Strengthening of the immune system
D. Decreased muscle tension
E. Decreased heart rate and blood pressure
F. Improved circulation

A. Change in Brain Wave Activity

Studies indicate that the electrical activity of the brain produces waves that can be measured with an electroencephalogram (EEG). Through electrodes attached to the scalp, the EEG measures the electrical activity of the brain cells. The results appear on a graph that records the different types of brain waves. There are four types of waves: beta, alpha, theta, and delta.

Brain Waves:

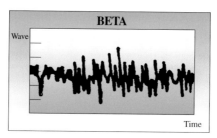

Beta waves: Rapid waves with low electrical force. These waves occur when we are awake, active, and aware of external stimuli.

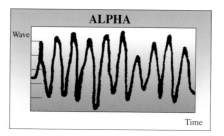

Alpha waves: Slow waves with a high electrical force. Alpha waves occur when we are relaxed. Their presence calms the brain, makes it more receptive, and increases concentration, efficiency and creativity.

Theta waves: Theta waves occur during the first stage of sleep.

Delta waves: Delta waves occur during deep sleep.

At this very moment, as you read these words, or while using your five senses in every day life, the brain is primarily producing beta waves. These waves occur during reading, talking, listening, writing, etc.

When you close your eyes and perform a relaxation exercise you disregard external stimuli and listen instead to what is happening inside your body. When you do this, the brain waves slow down and their strength increases. These are alpha waves.

American researcher Jose Silva, creator of the Silva Method, discovered that in a state of relaxation there is increased alpha wave activity in the brain.

The brain is divided into two hemispheres. Each hemisphere grasps reality differently. The left hemisphere takes in information analytically, with great detail. It is thus characterized by a logical, systematic linear way of thinking, and is related to short-term memory.

The right hemisphere receives information globally and comprehensively. It conveys information to us in a concurrent manner, through pictures. This is the world of creative thinking, mental imagery, dreams, and long-term memory.

To illustrate the different ways in which each side of the brain takes in information, think of the following well-known allegory: Three blind men encounter an elephant for the first time in their lives. The one who grabs the elephant's tail thinks he is holding a rope. The one who touches the elephant's trunk thinks he has a snake in his hand. The third blind man feels the elephant's leg and is sure it is a tree trunk. Each of the blind men perceives a different component and does not receive the full picture.

The Functioning of the Brain

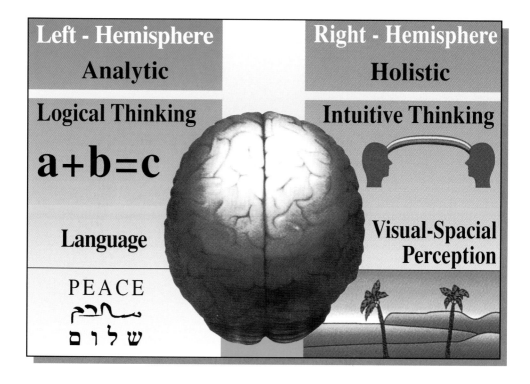

This is how the left hemisphere of the brain operates by taking in details and attempting to construct the entire picture based on them. The right hemisphere, in contrast, does not construct the whole from its parts, but grasps the picture just as a person who is not blind would see the elephant. The right hemisphere sees the elephant at once in its entirety, even putting together information that goes beyond the scope of vision, such as sensing the elephant's massive size and weight. In short, the right hemisphere perceives a simultaneous picture of most of the details.

You can take advantage of all the abilities in your brain only when you integrate the systematic thinking of the left hemisphere with the global grasp and intuitive flashes of the right hemisphere.

When the brain is producing more alpha waves, both hemispheres are synchronized. Under this ideal situation you can find solutions to problems and create new ideas. In this state, as opposed to a beta-wave state, there is balance between the two sides of the brain. As a result, the brain grasps more, and is more focused and creative. During an alpha state, your health improves, and your degree of fear diminishes, while the ability to see with your mind's eye increases, and memory is sharpened together with your learning ability.

In summary, some skills are used when you're in touch with the external world (the brain operating in beta), and others when you're in touch with your internal world, in a state of relaxation (the brain operating in alpha).

B. Decreased Respiration Rate

Rapid breathing is related to tension and excitement. The deeper the relaxation, the slower and more regular the breathing. In a state of relaxation, breathing is from the abdomen, and more air enters the lungs.

C. Strengthening of The Immune System

The immune system protects the body against germs, viruses and bacteria, which endanger our health. The leukocytes (white blood cells) form the basic cells of the immune system. They are produced in three parts of our body: the lymph nodes, the spleen and the bone marrow (the lymphocytes that stay in the bone marrow are called Bone Marrow B cells, and those that reach the thymus gland are called T cells).

When the leukocytes identify an intruder, they swallow it if it is small, or destroy it if it is large, by means of special proteins called antibodies. When we are sick there is a significant increase in the number of leukocytes enabling the body to better cope with the illness. When the body operates under stress, the adrenal gland generates hormones called glucocorticoids that suppress the production of antibodies and interfere with the action of the lymphocytes. The immune system becomes weaker. By contrast, in a state of relaxation the glucocorticoids are released in small quantities, enabling the lymphocytes to better protect the body against illness.

Lymphocytes Overcoming Cancerous Cells

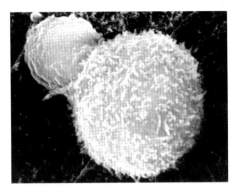

Above, a T cell, a lymphocyte from the thymus, attacks a cancerous cell (the large circle). Below, the cancerous cell disintegrates.

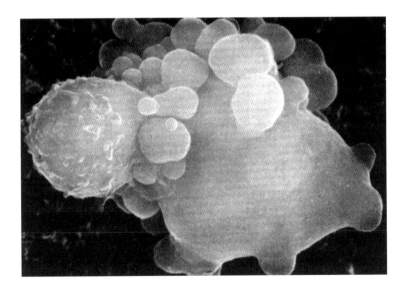

Andrejs Liepins of the Sloan-Kettering Institute took these micro-pictures for cancer research. We are grateful to the publisher, Edaf S.A., Spain, for allowing us to reproduce these photographs from the book *Kinesiología del Comportamiento* by Dr. John Diamond.

D. Decreased Muscle Tension

Relaxation exercises bring about a decrease in muscle tension. Through relaxation you can eliminate the pain of muscle cramps as well as learn how to relax and contract the muscles to the extent desired.

E. Decreased Heart Rate and Blood Pressure

Mental calm decreases heart rate. As the beat slows, the blood vessels expand, enabling more blood and oxygen to reach the heart. Expansion of the blood vessels helps lower blood pressure. Relaxation also reduces the amount of cholesterol in the blood and helps prevent its accumulation in the vessels.

F. Improved Circulation

Relaxation contributes to better blood circulation, and prevents blood viscosity and the tendency for blood to coagulate quickly. This stops the development of blood clots that could lead to thrombosis.

Psychological Effects of Relaxation

Relaxation has a significant psychological impact. Through relaxation, we can improve specific aspects of our personality, strengthening the positive qualities and changing unwanted habits and attitudes.

In a state of relaxation, various physical phenomena occur which are accompanied by a sense of repose and pleasure. These feelings reinforce emotional stability because in a state of relaxation we react calmly and reasonably to stress and adjust more easily to new situations. Our disposition is therefore more stable, and we are less given to mood swings.

In addition, relaxation brings about a positive change in our way of thinking, directing us towards a more open approach. By practicing relaxation, we take control of our reactions even under tension, and this strengthens our self-confidence and self-esteem. All these positive changes are recorded in our inner consciousness and automatically affect the way we react to stimuli.

The Effects of Stress

Physiological Effects

- The brain secretes harmful chemicals (corticotrophin)
- The mouth becomes dry
- The immune system is weakened
- Breathing becomes more rapid
- The muscles become tense
- The heart beats faster
- Blood pressure increases
- Digestion slows down

Psychological Effects

- Distress
- Lack of self-confidence
- Low self-esteem
- Relationship difficulties
- Aggressiveness
- Loss of emotional control
- Inability to concentrate

The Effects of Relaxation

Physiological Effects

- The brain produces more alpha waves which induce mental calmness
- Breathing slows down
- The immune system is strengthened
- Tension in the muscles eases
- The heart rate decreases
- Blood pressure drops
- Cholesterol levels decrease
- Blood circulation increases

Psychological Effects

- Feeling of ease
- Enhanced self-confidence
- Greater self-esteem
- More successful relationships
- Calmness
- Emotional control
- Good concentration

3
Anyone Can Achieve Relaxation

CHAPTER 3

Anyone Can Achieve Relaxation

Relaxation is a skill
acquired with practice.

The "12-Minute Pause"

The *"12-Minute Pause"* can be used by anyone who wants to enjoy the many benefits of relaxation. This exercise is set to original music written by Noam Atlas that enhances the sense of relaxation.

The combination of relaxation exercises and music on this CD allows you to obtain the maximum benefit from the exercise.

Optimal Conditions for Practicing the "12-Minute Pause"

Before beginning the *"12-Minute Pause"* give some thought to:

- your mental attitude
- where to do the exercise
- the optimal time of day
- frequency of exercise
- duration of exercise
- position of your body

The following conditions will enhance your results:

Mental Attitude

To benefit the most from this exercise, adopt a positive mental attitude and open yourself to the idea that you are able to achieve relaxation. Some people resist the idea of relaxing. Perhaps this has to do with a fear of losing control in a new and unfamiliar situation. However, relaxation is accomplished with your complete awareness and control, and you can terminate the exercise at any moment.

The secret to success is merely allowing yourself to relax. Most kinds of learning require an effort. To reach relaxation, however, you do not exert yourself. In fact, exertion hinders relaxation. It is impossible to command your body, "Relax yourself!" Only through your imagination can the body be brought to a state of relaxation.

What to Think About

Focus your attention on things that help you relax. Some will be external, such as the voice of the instructor and the background music, and some will be internal, such as the mental pictures you create and the pleasurable sensations you feel in your body that are associated with relaxation.

Following the recorded instructions, consider every part of your body and, using your imagination, create a pleasant feeling of weight, lightness, warmth, or the sensation of a certain limb being wider, softer, or looser, as you choose.

The more deeply you relax, the more you will become unaware of external noise. Although you will continue to hear outside noises, you'll be able to distinguish between the peacefulness inside of you and the noise from the outside.

With this exercise, you will reach physical and mental relaxation. Before you try it for the first time, it's a good idea to read the section "Doing the Exercise" and to listen to the CD the *"12-Minute Pause"* once through so that you'll be familiar with its contents.

Where to Do It

Choose a quiet and pleasant place for the exercise, some place where you won't be disturbed. This is especially important the first few times you practice it. After you gain some experience, you'll be able to reach a high level of relaxation even under less favorable conditions.

When to Do It

Do the exercise at the easiest and most convenient time of day for you. All hours of the day are suitable for relaxation. It is important, however, to set a regular exercise hour, in order to have relaxation become a habit.

How Often to Do It

Relaxation is a skill that can be acquired only through practice. Therefore, it's a good idea to do the exercise at least once a day. If that is too much for you, practicing several times a week will also enable you to benefit from relaxation.

If you have health or medical problems, practice the *"12-Minute Pause"* three times a day in addition to your medical treatment.

The Position of Your Body

We recommend that you do the exercise while seated on a chair or on a comfortable couch and not while laying on a bed. It is too easy to fall asleep in bed, and that is not the aim of the exercise.

The purpose of the exercise is to reach a state in which the muscles are relaxed at the same time that the brain is alert and active. Therefore the exercise should be performed while you are sitting in a comfortable position, leaning back in a chair, your hands resting on your thighs, with the palms either facing down or up, the balls of your feet resting on the floor, and your legs and feet uncrossed.

How Long Does It Take?

The exercise lasts for 12 minutes. This is a short amount of time to devote to it, but long enough to allow you to learn relaxation and to reap its benefits.

Potential Concerns During the Exercise

The first few times you do the exercise, you might feel some stiffness in the nape of your neck, your shoulders, or various other parts of your body. This is body tension which sometimes manifests itself when you begin the process of relaxation.

This is similar to what happens to you when you first take up physical exercise. Initially, your whole body aches, but after a while you feel the positive effects of exercise. In relaxation, too, the way to overcome initial discomfort is by continuing the exercise. Only through regular exercise can you release the overstress.

If you have low blood pressure, you may feel a slight dizziness if you come out of the exercise too quickly or stand up immediately after doing it. We suggest that you withdraw gradually from the exercise by moving your body slowly, opening your eyes, and gradually returning to regular activity.

We also suggest that you eat something light before the exercise, because if you haven't eaten for several hours, you may experience a decrease in your blood sugar level. On the other hand, you should not do the exercise right after eating a large meal because you could become drowsy and fall asleep. That wouldn't be terrible, but as we said, it's not the point of the exercise.

Some people may feel their heart beating when doing the exercise. This is merely because they are paying greater attention to what is going on inside of the body. If you start worrying that your heart may be beating too fast, you will cause an increase in the level of adrenaline in the blood, which stimulates the heart to pump even harder! Just calm down. When you relax, your heart rate slows down. It will not speed up.

If during the exercise you feel the need to move or scratch yourself, it's better to get it over with and then go on with the exercise. If distracting thoughts enter your mind, let them slip in and out naturally, then go back to concentrating on the exercise.

Note that if you feel uncomfortable at any time during the exercise, you can stop. You're in complete control. You can always count to 3, open your eyes, and come out of the relaxation exercise. You can repeat the exercise at another time, until it becomes a pleasurable and refreshing habit.

The first few times you do the exercise, you might not yet feel any positive results in your body.

First, don't worry about whether or not you did the exercises correctly. Naturally, sometimes you reach a better state of relaxation than others.

Second, don't give up! Over time, all the desirable signs will appear: heaviness, lightness, a light, pleasant warmth, warmth in your fingers, slower breathing and a slower heart rate, concentration, alertness, an overall good feeling, and many other sensations. The moment you feel a change toward the desired direction, try to reconstruct what you felt, what you thought, and what you imagined at that moment so you can recreate that pleasant feeling during future exercises. You have to let go of the idea of "all or nothing." Some people think "I'm either relaxed or in a state of stress." You will gradually be able to reach different levels of relaxation. The very fact that you're doing the exercise is an important step on your path to relaxation. Relaxation is a skill acquired with practice. You will gradually become better and better at relaxing.

We emphasize the fact that relaxation has a cumulative effect. Every relaxation exercise you do will help you reach relaxation more easily. You'll be able to feel the positive and cumulative effects of the exercise even after it's over.

Doing the Exercise

To begin the exercise, sit in a comfortable position, put on the earphones if you are using them, turn on the CD, and close your eyes.

We begin the exercise with eyes closed because we produce a greater number of alpha waves in the brain which in turn help us relax. Then follow the recorded instructions.

In the first part of the exercise you'll be given instructions on how to loosen up your body, limb by limb, to reach physical relaxation. You can concentrate on the part of the body you want to relax. Feel it becoming softer and more limp, flexible and loose, and notice the pleasant sensation slowly spreading through your body.

When you relax your neck muscles, the head tends to nod forward and you feel your hands and feet becoming either heavier or lighter. You might also feel a light, tingling warmth. This is a pleasant feeling that comes from improved circulation of blood when you are relaxed.

After you attain physical relaxation and feel your body loose and relaxed, you'll be asked to focus on peaceful images to achieve mental relaxation.

You will be told to stroll through a forest and enjoy the scenery in all its details. You have to use your imagination and feel that you are actually in the forest. Then, you will be asked to go into your personal place of relaxation. The object is to imagine yourself in either a real place that you are familiar with, or some imaginary place that you create.

The ideas you'll be given and the special background music will help you create this personal place for yourself.

Your creative imagination will be called upon for visualizing your special place with all its details. You will see, feel, hear, smell, and taste, just as if you are actually there. If you choose the seashore, for example, you see yourself walking along the beach (sight); you feel the sand under your feet, the sun warming your shoulders, the breeze blowing in from the sea (touch); you hear the cawing of the sea gulls and the waves breaking on the shore (sound); and you breathe in the special fragrance of the sea (smell). While walking, you enjoy a refreshing ice cream in your favorite flavor (taste).

Using all of the senses in your personal place of relaxation helps you focus on the image, keeping other thoughts or anxieties at bay. As a result, you reach a higher plane of concentration and mental relaxation. Even if you don't manage to utilize all of your senses, the very thought of being there will have a beneficial effect. The more you practice, the more easily you'll be able to evoke additional sensations.

You will have a minute to rest in your personal place of relaxation. During this time you will see and feel it deeply, absorbing its special atmosphere. When the minute is up, you may feel that much more time has passed, and you will feel peaceful and serene.

After reaching physical and mental relaxation, the instructions will help you conclude the exercise by slowly counting to three. You'll feel good, wide awake, and ready for your daily routine.

Good luck!

Monitoring Your Progress

Learning relaxation can be accomplished only through practice. To monitor your progress, we have prepared a questionnaire that you can fill in after each exercise.

Personal Questionnaire for Monitoring Progress

You'll find items in the questionnaire that describe phenomena and feelings which occurred during the exercise; some are more positive than others. After doing the *"12-Minute Pause,"* review the 15 items in the questionnaire and respond as follows!

Yes – **(Y)**
Partly – **(P)**
No – **(N)**

Mark one of these answers for each item for a full picture of your progress.

Personal Questionnaire for Monitoring Results

No.	Item
1.	During the exercise I felt a heaviness or lightness in my limbs.
2.	I felt my breathing slow down.
3.	I fell asleep during the exercise.
4.	I managed to follow the instructions.
5.	I felt distracted during the exercise.
6.	I felt my whole body limp and loose.
7.	I felt at ease and pleasantly calm.
8.	I was able to see my personal place in great detail.
9.	I felt warmth in my hands.
10.	I felt tired after the exercise.
11.	I felt alert and refreshed.
12.	During the exercise I became restless.
13.	I managed to overcome any anxiety during the exercise.
14.	I didn't feel anything special.
15.	I feel more relaxed.

After completing the *"12-Minute Pause,"* fill in the "Answer" column with your response to each of the 15 items:
Yes (Y)   Partly (P)   No (N)

Item	Exercise 1		Exercise 2		Exercise 3		Exercise 4		Exercise 5		Exercise 6	
No.	Answer	Score	Answer	Score	Answer	Score	Answer	Score	Answer	Score	Answer	Score
1.												
2.												
3.												
4.												
5.												
6.												
7.												
8.												
9.												
10.												
11.												
12.												
13.												
14.												
15.												
Total												

After marking your answer to the 15 items, check the conversion table on the next page and fill in the score for each item above.

Conversion Table

Item No.	Yes	Partly	No.
1.	2	1	0
2.	2	1	0
3.	0	1	2
4.	2	1	0
5.	0	1	2
6.	2	1	0
7.	2	1	0
8.	2	1	0
9.	2	1	0
10.	0	1	2
11.	0	1	0
12.	2	1	2
13.	0	1	0
14.	0	1	2
15.	2	1	0

1. For each item find the "score" (point value) in the conversion table above, and mark it next to your answer. For example, if your answer to item no. 1 was "yes," give yourself a score of 2; for "partly," score 1; for "no," score 0.
2. Add up all the scores for the exercise and mark the sum in the box for "Total."
3. Move on to the table "Explanation of the Total Score."

Explanation of the Total Score

0-9	You haven't yet achieved relaxation.
10-15	You've made a start.
16-21	You have achieved relaxation.
22-27	You're practicing good relaxation.
28-30	You've made it. Excellent relaxation level!

15 points or less: Don't give up! Continue the exercise regularly and your achievements will undoubtedly improve.

Between 16 and 21 points: Good. You have learned how to achieve relaxation. Now keep up the exercise to reach an even higher level of relaxation.

22 points or higher: Congratulations!

4
The Benefits of Relaxation

CHAPTER 4

The Benefits of Relaxation

Exercises and practical tips that will help make relaxation work for you.

In the following pages we'll describe more in depth the many benefits of relaxation. This section is filled with helpful information, exercises, and practical tips that will help make relaxation work for you.

Relaxation Releases Tension

One of the first benefits that you will notice when you begin to practice relaxation is a significantly lower level of tension. Even after only a few practice exercises, you will feel calmer and more peaceful.

Relaxation Helps Reduce Accumulated Tension

When you pick up a sleeping infant, you feel the entire weight of its body in your arms, fully relaxed, without a trace of tension. Every healthy baby is born with the ability to relax completely.

As we grow older, we "learn" to contract our muscles. Each time we contract a muscle we use energy. Any muscle contraction which is not intended for a positive purpose is a waste of energy. A cat, for example, keeps its legs limp when they aren't in use. When a cat springs into action, it flexes its legs to the precise extent required, no more and no less.

Often, we contract our muscles and keep them that way for no purpose, especially when reacting to thoughts and feelings.

For example, if a person is criticized or given a high-pressure task to perform, his shoulders stiffen, the nape of his neck tightens, and his face muscles harden into a strained and angry look. These physical reactions use up energy, and if the muscles remain contracted for a long period of time, important energy is wasted that could have been available for daily functioning.

Anxieties, frustrations, and fears precipitate a similar contraction of the muscles. That is why it's not surprising that after a day's work, we feel more tired than we should!

Relaxation is the most natural, beneficial, and effective way to overcome the negative effects of accumulated stress in the body and to restore its energy.

Relaxation for Coping with Stressful Situations

Some real life situations such as illness, work difficulties or problems in relationships bring about stress. Young people who are about to enter college, or those who have just graduated, experience tension because they are about to cope with a new situation that demands considerable adjustment. Retiring from work is another situation of extreme change in which an individual, overnight, is divested of habitual stimuli, activity, and responsibility. Retired people whose work was the central focus of their lives experience tremendous stress. Early retirement in particular requires the individual to find an alternative occupation and to begin struggling anew.

When relaxation is practiced over a long period of time, one's negative reaction to stressful factors decreases due to an anti-stress reaction that sets in (caused by reduced activity in the limbic system* and the hypothalamus.) As a result, the person reacts to the stressful factors in a cooler, more collected manner.

Reacting calmly is beneficial to various aspects of our personality

- Greater emotional stability (less impulsive behavior and fewer mood swings)
- A tendency to focus our control internally (based on the belief that the positive and negative elements in our lives can be controlled through behavior)
- Enhanced self-esteem (as a result of feeling in control)

Practicing relaxation on a regular basis reinforces these changes, and helps us better cope with stressful situations.

---

* The limbic system monitors emotions and controls our basic drives such as for food, sex, and survival.

Relaxation is Physically Beneficial and Improves Health

Today it is universally acknowledged that many ailments are brought on by stress. Therefore, reducing stress is the first step to preventing illnesses.

The body is capable of healing itself in the most efficient way possible, as long as the mind is free of stress and allows it to perform its job. We can help the body heal through positive thoughts, relaxation, rest, proper nutrition and physical activity.

Blood tests can indicate if an individual is healthy or sick. The condition of the blood depends on several factors:

What we are thinking about
How we breathe
What we eat and drink

Thoughts, however, are the primary factor. Changing our diet without changing our thoughts, for example, will have little effect.

Many studies have shown that negative expectations impede the healing process, while positive expectations contribute to better health (a typical "self-fulfilling prophecy").

People who are ill or about to undergo an operation often develop negative thoughts.
"I won't survive this" or, "this treatment won't help" are some of the negative thoughts often heard.
These thoughts and their accompanying mental images convey a negative message to the brain. The brain passes this message on

to the immune system: "Don't bother exerting yourself, it won't help anyway!"

Relaxation can help surmount these negative expectations, because negative thoughts cannot survive in a state of relaxation. Fear dissipates when the muscles are loose. When a person is relaxed, recuperation from illness can be significantly faster.

A new field in advanced medicine, psycho-neuro-immunology, is based on studies showing that the neurotransmitters (which transfer messages between nerve cells) are linked to our immunological system. This means that thinking, feeling, and healing are interrelated functions. they are closely and mutually connected.

When we experience fear or pain, it affects each and every cell of the body. Emotions can impede the flow of neurotransmitters resulting in a disorder, anything from a headache to cancer. Fortunately, positive emotions also affect the neurotransmitters in strengthening the body and improving our health.

Everyone has some moments in life in which he or she would like to be able to recover quickly from a pain or an ailment. The first advantage of relaxation is that it expedites the process of physical healing. This is due to the automatic healing mechanisms that function better in a state of relaxation. Therefore, if you have health problems, do the *"12-Minute Pause"* three times a day at the most convenient hours for you (for example, in the morning after you wake up, in the afternoon, and at night before retiring).

After doing the *"12-Minute Pause"* several times, you'll be able to relax without the CD, and to use the exercise below for improving your health.

Exercise for Improving Health

Close your eyes and remember the same physical sensations throughout your body that you feel when you do *the "12-Minute Pause."* Relax from head to toe, just as you do during that exercise. Take a deep breath and hold it for several seconds.

During this time, imagine that your breath is energy, and picture it in any form you like – a ray of light, for example.

As you exhale the air, you can convey this energy to any part of your body that needs it.

Imagine yourself conveying the breath of air, that is now energy, to a specific part of your body. Feel the area filling up with strength and vitality. You can imagine, for example, that the limb is becoming bigger or more colorful. You feel a gentle tingling, or that the entire area fills with light (these are images that the brain identifies with healing).

Every time you feel these sensations, the natural defense mechanisms of your body will begin to work more efficiently, enhancing your health.

If you need surgery, perform the *"12-Minute Pause"* three times a day until the operation takes place, in order to build up your body's defenses and lower the level of stress and fear. Doing these exercises three times a day after the operation will also facilitate your recuperation.

For cancer, you can achieve a state of relaxation on your own and see, in your mind's eye, how the white blood cells of your immune system prevail over the cancerous cells. Look at the photographs on page 51 that document the struggle between the thymus cells (T cells) and the unhealthy cells.

Our immune system identifies and destroys all cancerous cells that our bodies produce. Certain people develop cancer because of their genetic make-up. The mind, however, can also play an active role in developing or impeding cancer.

When a person is diagnosed with cancer, it means that the immune system has failed to function properly and that it should be activated.

Many cases of spontaneous recovery occur when the immune system is reactivated.

Dr. Andrew Weil one of the leading American doctors in the field of body and mind relationships, claims that there are cases in which the immune system has been suddenly activated and can dissolve the cancer tumor in a few hours or days (Weil,1995). Such was the case of the sister of a Silva Method graduate, whose story was on Israeli TV in the movie "Meetings with Jose." The woman was diagnosed by three different doctors as having breast cancer. Her sister tells the story:

> I told her not to do anything before coming to
> visit me in Jerusalem where she could see my
> doctor whom I have known and trusted for

many years. When we consulted him, he said 'I'm sorry, but it is cancer. 'He wanted to operate immediately, but we asked him to wait until the following day. We went home and I introduced my sister to the Silva Method. She did all the exercises under my guidance. We always have had a very strong relationship. We practiced all night long and the next morning we went back to the doctor. When he examined her, he could not believe it. He said, 'If I hadn't seen the tumor yesterday, I would have never believed something like this could happen. The tumor has disappeared.'

Dr. Weil's observations are exemplified in this case. The Silva Method exercises triggered the immune system, which in turn dissolved the cancerous cells within hours.

The patient's sister concludes, "We need to be able to concentrate, to think clearly and positively. It was not a miracle. It has to do with working and connecting ourselves with the right sources. I don't believe in supernatural miracles. I believe in the power of individuals to make miracles happen for themselves."

Dr. Deepak Chopra (1989) also does not think that we are dealing with miracles. The mind can persuade our consciousness to fight against the disease, and through the immune system we can make the change happen ourselves.

Modern science claims that our mind – its feelings, wishes and beliefs – are the result of chemical processes that occur inside the body's molecules. Dr. Chopra, as well as many other researchers, believes that the opposite is true. He states that we are made up of a network of intelligence, which knows how to create the physical body. It means that each cell in our physical body carries within itself both energy and intelligence, enabling it to change the patterns that build the body and correct the malignant cells.

Our body is capable of continually renewing itself. In less than a year, all the body's cells, except for the brain cells, are renewed. Certain cells renew very quickly. For example, the stomach cells take only a few days, while others take longer: skin cells renew themselves in one month, skeletal cells are renewed within three months.

Dr. Chopra claims that cancer cells also renew themselves, but the cells' memory remains the same. Hence, even the new cells continue to produce the tumor. In order to change this situation, the memory and the energy contained within the cell should be modified.

Dr. Carl Simonton (1975) supports the concept that the body can cure itself from cancer. Relaxation is the best state of mind with which one can fight cancer. In this state of mind it is easy to direct thoughts, as well as to open one's self to new messages, to eliminate worries, and to prepare the body for efficiently correcting any anomaly. Dr. Simonton found that patients who knew how to reach relaxation and were able to imagine how the strong cells of the immune system fought against the weak cancerous cells, could actually increase their chances of recovery.

The state of relaxation contributes to a change in attitude, creates positive expectations and strengthens the will to recover, enabling the immune system to produce the proper chemical modifications.

It is very important to remember that our beliefs have the power to control chemical reactions in our bodies and that therefore adapting a new, positive belief can instantly bring about a chemical modification. The chemical materials that inhibit or encourage our immune system depend on the negative or positive beliefs we hold.

Dr. Yigal Harpaz, a graduate of the Silva Method course who used our techniques to cure himself from a severe liver disease, tells his story:

> In 1979, my liver began a quick process of deterioration as a result of a disease for which conventional medicine had found no explanation. The best doctors defined my state as terminal. During all the stages of the illness I continued to be optimistic, even when I understood that the doctors considered my condition as critical. I decided to fight for my life. How? By using mental exercises.
>
> While staying in the hospital, I lay in my bed with my eyes closed. I imagined that I could see my malfunctioning liver on a TV screen. I compared it to the drainage system of a big town, which had failed and could not operate. In order to fix the problem, someone had to dig deep down and stabilize the ground by cementing it. I then imagined my destroyed liver cells as the pipes that needed fixing, and the medicines as the cement that could stabilize my liver.
>
> While picturing this image, I felt itching along my liver which was accompanied by a slight

vibration. This phenomenon repeated itself as long as I continued these exercises. The feeling would stop as soon as I stopped doing them. At the end of the first week I could see that the entire central pipe had been dug out and that the stagnated liquids were being drained. At the same time, I felt as if the great pressure in my liver had been released. And indeed, on that same day, the doctors found signs indicating that my liver had started to function normally again. I continued practicing the exercises for several more days until I recovered from the illness.

As Dr. Herbert Benson (1996) claims, "beliefs can be a major source of illness and a major force in treatment."

Relaxation Lowers Blood Pressure and Helps Prevent Heart Problems

Many people begin paying attention to their health only after they've had a serious problem, such as a heart attack. Relaxation can be of help after the attack, but it can also serve as preventive treatment. It is well known that high blood pressure can cause heart attack. High blood pressure can be the result of organic factors (infections, accidents, poisoning) or psychological factors (overpowering emotions, fears). Studies show that the mind can lower high blood pressure.

The heart is very susceptible to mental influence. Strong emotions, anger, and aggressiveness, can increase heartbeat and raise blood pressure. A famous British surgeon used to say, "My life is in the hands of every fool who angers me." (This man died of a heart attack in the middle of a stormy meeting at the hospital.)

How Relaxation Can Help If You Have High Blood Pressure or Heart Disease

The relaxation exercise reduces the heart rate so that the heart pumps less. The blood vessels of the heart expand, improving blood circulation and allowing for a better supply of oxygen to the cells and tissues of the body.

With relaxation, blood pressure is reduced, even from the very first exercises. However, only if you practice the *"12-Minute Pause"* on a regular basis, will the decrease in blood pressure become stable and permanently significant.

Medical research (Benson, 1975) has shown that during relaxation, blood pressure decreases only for persons suffering from hypertension (high blood pressure). No changes were found among subjects with normal or low blood pressure.

We now present an exercise that will help blood vessels expand and lower blood pressure:

Exercise for Lowering Blood Pressure

After you have practiced the *"12-Minute Pause,"* you can reach relaxation on your own.

Close your eyes and remember the same physical sensations throughout your body that you feel when you do the *"12-Minute Pause."* Relax your body from head to toe just as you do during

that exercise. Then visualize yourself in your personal place of relaxation

With your mind's eye, perceive the blood vessels connected to your heart. They are expanding and becoming more flexible. Their circumference is increasing and blood is flowing through them easily. Look at a blood pressure gauge and see how the needle falls to the safe green zone.

You know that the more relaxed you are, the more you can control your blood pressure and your emotional reactions. You feel calm and open-minded. Picture yourself having good relationships with others. You are able to cope with your tension and to solve problems easily in any situation.

Relaxation is Beneficial for the Respiratory System

After physical exertion, breathing is rapid and the upper part of the chest expands and contracts. Excitable people who tend to over-react under normal situations breathe like this all the time. Slow, rhythmic breathing introduces more air into the lungs, which subsequently increases lung capacity and volume.

When we are relaxed and breathe from the abdomen, the diaphragm (the muscle under the ribcage) massages the abdomen, making the muscles feel relaxed. Release of the diaphragm, the rib muscles and the abdominal muscles, enlarges chest capacity.

Athletes who require extraordinary respiration capacity can derive great benefit from relaxation. Similarly, people suffering from asthma, bronchitis, and other respiratory diseases will also feel relief from their condition following relaxation exercises.

Relaxation also reduces the fear that often accompanies diseases of the respiratory tract.

If you suffer from breathing problems, we suggest that you practice the *"12-Minute Pause"* three times a day.

Relaxation is Beneficial for the Digestive System

Do you suffer from constipation, diarrhea, or stomach aches? Relaxation exercises might help you. When we are in a state of stress, food remains in the stomach a longer time (6 hours instead of 4, and sometimes up to 24 hours!). Relaxation soothes the entire system and facilitates digestion. Relaxation releases the abdominal muscles and allows them to carry out digestive activity, calming all of the organs in both the upper and lower abdominal area.

Relaxation Alleviates Stress-Related Pains

As noted earlier, we often keep muscles contracted for no reason, as a response to thoughts and emotions. Negative thoughts and emotions manifest themselves in particular places throughout the body (one's most vulnerable points) in the form of chronic muscle cramps. For example, a young boy whose mother is constantly telling him that "men don't cry" will try to hold back his tears by contracting the chin muscles. Over time, his chin muscles will become chronically contracted.

Another example: A woman who is sensitive to criticism automatically contracts the muscles at the nape of her neck any time she is criticized. If this woman hears criticism frequently, these muscles will be contracted often, and over time they will remain contracted.

Frequently, the muscles of the neck, the nape, the back, and the shoulders remain contracted because of stress. As a result, we suffer headaches, backaches, and pains in the shoulders or legs. These pains will disappear only when the level of tension is reduced. Through relaxation we learn to release these cramped muscles, eliminate the pains caused by tension, and even prevent them from recurring. As you practice the *"12-Minute Pause,"* you will discover that the pain that had been with you for so long, has disappeared. You have completely cured that part of your body!

Relaxation Enriches Daily Functioning

In day to day life, we must cope with commitments, decision-making, and problems of all sorts: financial, health, interpersonal, work-related, and the like. The higher the level of stress, the harder it is for us to make decisions and successfully cope.

This is where relaxation comes to our rescue. Relaxation is most important for daily functioning. It has a beneficial, enriching effect on our emotions and thoughts, helping us sleep better, dissipating fatigue, fostering better personal relationships, increasing work productivity, sharpening concentration and memory, enhancing self-confidence, and improving sexual performance. We will consider all these aspects in the coming pages.

Relaxation Has a Beneficial Effect on Emotions and Thoughts

Emotions and thoughts affect the body. Thought tends to turn into action, whether we actually carry it out or merely imagine it. The Russian physician Ivan P. Pavlov proved that mental images can affect muscle activity, breathing rate, and the chemistry of the blood. For his research on reflexes, Pavlov was awarded the Nobel Prize. Each time he gave food to the dogs in his experiment, he rang a bell. After some time, the dogs began to salivate whenever they heard the bell, regardless of whether or not they received food. Pavlov thus uncovered the conditioned reflex. The dogs "imagined" the food and salivated whenever the bell rang.

We invite you to experience the effect that the imagination can produce. Read the following lines slowly, and let your imagination flow with the words:

Picture a small lemon, fragrant and juicy. Examine its yellow color and feel its smooth skin. Bring it to your nose and smell it. Inhale the wonderful and tantalizing aroma. Now take a knife and cut the lemon in half. Squeeze one half of the lemon straight into your mouth. Feel the sour taste of the lemon on your tongue, the tangy juice filling your mouth.

Did you feel the saliva in your mouth? That was an actual physical reaction to an imaginary lemon. Using the same technique, blood circulation can be increased to all parts of the body if you concentrate on it. Everyone knows that we can turn pale from fear, or red from anger or shame. These changes are caused by the flow of blood in the blood vessels of the head and neck – decreased in the case of paleness and increased when we flush. Fear or excitement speeds up the heartbeat. All of these phenomena reflect the effect of thoughts on the body. We can prove that imagination causes reactions within the body through an experiment that uses a pendulum.

A pendulum is a weight hung at the end of a string. The string is held between the thumb and the forefinger.

If you have never observed this phenomenon, we suggest that you obtain a pendulum or simply make one by hanging a ring or button at the end of a string.

Take a piece of paper and draw two straight lines that intersect, one horizontal and the other vertical. Hold the pendulum's string in your hand and rest your elbow on the table. Hold the pendulum an inch or so above the intersection of the two lines.

While relaxed, think that you want the pendulum to move along the horizontal line. Don't physically move the pendulum with your fingers. You just have to want it to move. Before long, the pendulum will begin to move in the direction desired.

Every mental image (visual, aural, tactile, and emotional) affects the physiology of the body. Imagination activates the body. If you imagine that you are lifting something heavy off the floor, you will contract the appropriate muscles to perform that exertion.

When you imagined the lemon, you began to salivate. The body reacts the same way whether the lemon is real or imaginary. This happens because the brain does not differentiate between a real experience and an imaginary one. This fact is of utmost importance because we're constantly imagining things that affect our bodies, as if they were a reality. If we usually imagine good things, the outcome will be very different than if we imagine negative things.

If you placed a foot-wide board that was six feet long on the floor of your living room, would you be able to walk on it without difficulty? Of course. You could do it easily. However, if you placed that same board between two balconies, would you be able to walk on it as easily as you did when it was in your living room?

Naturally it would be much harder. What was so simple in the living room turns out to be a difficult, nerve-wracking task. Why? The reason is not physical; after all, it's the same board. What is happening is that you are telling yourself, "I have to be careful, I might fall," and then you feel fear. Our limitations come from negative messages created by the brain. Think what can happen when you imagine yourself healthy and happy.

It will undoubtedly have a beneficial effect on your body!

Relaxation can be used to neutralize negative feelings and help you reach emotional balance, enabling you to change attitudes and behavior in the desired direction.

Relaxation Promotes Restful Sleep and Dispels Fatigue

Relaxation can relieve many types of sleep disorders. Sleeping pills provide only temporary help at most. People who suffer from bronchitis or emphysema must avoid taking sleeping pills since they can suppress the respiratory system. Elderly people should also avoid sleeping pills because they cannot shake off their effect as readily as younger people. In many cases the elderly are somewhat confused after a dose of sleeping pills and are prone to falling and resultant bone fractures.

Through relaxation exercises, we can free ourselves of tension and wake up more refreshed. We will not feel fatigue during the day, and can even enjoy a tranquil night's sleep. Good relaxation helps us fall asleep easily and enables us to enjoy a deeper, higher-quality sleep. After regular practice of the *"12-Minute Pause,"* you will sleep better and may even need fewer hours of sleep.

Relaxation Promotes the Improvement of Relationships

When we are under stress our perceptions become distorted. An example of this idea is Dan when he was late for work. "Good morning," said a friend who popped into his office a few minutes after he arrived. Dan became angry with his friend, believing that the "Good morning" was intended to point out that Dan had come in late. The friend, however, had not even noticed.

Situations similar to this one happen frequently when we're under stress. On the other hand, when we're relaxed, we tend to think in a more logical, rational manner and to participate in situations without negative emotional involvement. As a result, our reactions are more balanced and we can even have a positive effect on persons around us who are agitated. Calm people radiate authority and can prevent other peoples' outbursts of anger.

The *"12-Minute Pause,"* will help you to develop better relationships. Regular practice of the exercise the *"12-Minute Pause"* on the CD will help you improve your overall mood and grant you the capacity for greater patience, tolerance, and empathy for others.

It's important to remember that for interpersonal relationships, the content of a conversation is less important than the emotional connection that is created. A week after you have a conversation with someone, you may not recall what was said. A year later, you may not recall that the conversation took place at all. But you are likely to remember the feeling you had toward that person. The emotional tie will remain, for better or for worse.

As you become calmer and more positive, your communication with others will be better.

Relaxation Improves Productivity of Managers and Employees

Work raises the stress level in different ways – high expectations, heavy responsibilities, competitiveness, over-exertion, heavy workloads, and long working hours. Business managers are particularly prone to this high pressure.

Stress can affect productivity at work. When you devote more time and energy to working, productivity increases, but only to a certain point. When you pass that point stress also increases. You don't have enough time to devote to other areas of your life – family, health, personal growth, leisure – and you lose a sense of balance in your life. The result is dissatisfaction and diminished productivity at work.

The *"12-Minute Pause"* will help you feel calmer. Regular use of the technique will enable you to dispel tension rather than accumulate it.

The ability to achieve relaxation is a valuable skill for all business people, even those who are already professionally successful. This is also true for workers and employees. For this reason, many companies in the United States, France, Japan, and Switzerland give their employees time to study and do relaxation exercises during the working day. Short breaks for relaxation during the day reduces accumulated physical and emotional stress. As a result, employee productivity increases significantly.

Furthermore, there's a long incubation period between the first signs of harmful tension and the manifestation of the ailment caused by stress. During this period you have the opportunity to step in and stop the ailment rather than ignoring signs of stress and allowing it to develop. This means that you can prevent the illnesses that most managers are prone to: heart attack, high blood pressure, and ulcers.

Perhaps you feel that 12 minutes is a great deal of your time because of your busy schedule. The moment you start following the exercise on a daily basis, however, you will feel the benefits of relaxation and discover that it is not a waste of time. In fact, you will ultimately be saving yourself time and energy and preventing future problems.

Perhaps you're so overwhelmed with things to do that you cannot follow the exercise. If that's the case, we suggest you take the following approach:

Immediate Repose

Under a high-pressure situation, all you have to do is envision your personal place for several seconds, and you'll instantly feel an easing of the tension and be able to better cope with the immediate demands.

How to Improve Interpersonal Relationships and to Cope with Work Pressures

The approach you have toward work can make it either easier or harder:

- Do you feel good about your work or occupation?

- Does the working day go by pleasantly, with you feeling in control of things? Or are you agitated and fearful about things that are going to happen?

- Do you have negative expectations, or do you assume that everything that happens to you will work out for the better?

Since most people spend much of their time at work, it is very important to improve inter-personal relationships and to cope positively with work pressures. Sometimes we think that we have no influence over the behavior of other people who bother us. The problem seems to be out of our control, and we feel that there is no way out – we can either suffer or quit. We can improve this situation, however, if we choose to change, starting first with ourselves.

We should be aware that those things which disturb us are not completely dependent on the situation itself, but on the meaning we attribute to it. No one can hurt us without our permission. The damage caused to us depends primarily on the extent to which we allow others to influence us. We should control our feelings and not permit any circumstances or people to hurt us or threaten our health.

A change in our behavior toward colleagues will bring about a change in their attitude toward us. There is no action without a reaction. If we continue to behave the way we always have, we will elicit and receive the same responses as always. If we change our behavior, people's reactions to us will also change accordingly.

If we cannot bring about a desired change of behavior in others, at least we can succeed in changing ourselves internally so that conflicts will not affect us in the same way as before.

Once we are no longer unreasonably involved emotionally, we are free to select the proper strategy to influence other people's behavior.

In the Silva Method course we learn a technique that can be used under similar situations – the "three fingers technique." We provide our brain with a sign to direct it toward a specific direction.

Join together three fingers from one hand (thumb, forefinger, and middle finger) and fold the ring finger and the little finger dawn to touch the palm. (See illustration). In order to make this sign meaningful, practice it when you are in a state of relaxation.

The Three Finger Exercise

After practicing the *"12-Minute Pause,"* close your eyes and relax your body from head to toe, just as you have done in the recorded exercise. Do it quickly, within a few minutes. Afterwards, envision yourself in your personal place. Tell yourself: "Anytime I join the three fingers together (practice doing it) I will control my feelings and react in a way which is best suited for me."

Repeat this exercise three times a day for one week. Then the three finger sign will hold some meaning for you, and you will be able to use it for your own purposes, not allowing other people's behavior to affect you negatively.

Anytime you face an unpleasant situation join these three fingers and your mind will receive the same message that you gave it during the week of exercises - "I will control my feelings and react in a way that is best suited for me."

Dr. Maxwell Maltz says that the first hour of the morning is the most important as it determines the rest of the day. If you begin the day feeling that everything will be fine, that you will connect well with people around you and have imaginative ideas, the chances increase that this will actually happen. To help your imagination create positive expectations we suggest a special exercise that you can do when you wake up in the morning.

Programming a Successful Day

Close your eyes and remember the same physical sensations throughout your body that you feel when you do the *"12-Minute Pause."* Relax your body from head to toe. Then envision yourself in your personal place of relaxation.

In your mind, go over everything that you'd like to do today. Think about what you'd like to accomplish in the course of the day. Imagine and feel that you're achieving all of these things, and that everything is going according to your expectations. Also, imagine your colleagues and the positive, agreeable connection you are creating with them. You feel great. You're succeeding and are in control.

Relaxation Sharpens Concentration, Memory and Learning Ability

Many people have to face tests and examinations, not just students at school or university but also candidates for certain positions, lecturers, politicians, insurance agents, merchants, and even people facing an important interview or meeting. Such situations can be very stressful, and some individuals even become ill from them.

Another well-known phenomenon is that of forgetting everything – blacking out – in the middle of an exam or in a high-stress situation. How does this happen?

The act of thinking is based on an electrical-chemical process that takes place between nerve cells. Two nerve cells communicate with each other through a chemical substance secreted onto the synapse (the junction where information is transmitted from one nerve cell to another). Stress increases the secretion of the adrenaline and noradrenaline hormones that reach the synapse, delaying or disrupting the transmission of information, and blocking the memory. This can be prevented through relaxation. Relaxation is a powerful tool that can ease stress and neutralize the high emotional charge inherent in any test.

Are you facing a situation that demands great concentration and especially a good memory? Is an important meeting or exam coming up? If so, you can and should prepare for it.

The night before the event and in the morning when you wake up, do the *"12-Minute Pause."*

While in a state of relaxation your heart will beat more slowly, your circulation will improve, more oxygen will reach the brain, and your body will rest, while your mind is active. As a result, there will be a marked improvement in your ability to concentrate and it will be easier to absorb material and remember the information that you need to do well on the test or in the meeting.

Suggestions for students:

When getting ready to study, you have to rid yourself of external and internal factors that distract you from the material. Eliminate the external factors by turning off the TV, asking those nearby not to disturb you, and unplugging the phone. As for internal factors, these include every type of negative internal dialogue, not just negative sentences you tell yourself, but also thoughts that distract you from your studies. These negative internal dialogues assume various forms. Some induce fear ("I don't have a good memory"; "I can't do it"); some foster failure ("I'm sure I won't pass the exam"); and others distract you from concentrating on your studies ("whom will I invite to my birthday party?").

Without a doubt, it's more pleasant to plan a party than to sit down and study. At a time like this, however, you have to choose between an immediate pleasure and the long-range pleasure. If you choose to study, thinking about other matters won't help. If you're calm, you'll have more control over the negative emotions that evoke fear or undermine your success, and it will be easier for you to concentrate on your studies and not escape to other occupations.

After studying for 40-45 minutes, take a relaxation break with the *"12-Minute Pause,"* which includes the subliminal message "I learn easily." Before returning to your studies, close your eyes for a moment and tell yourself, "I'm full of energy which will help me to study better."

How to Do Well on Examinations

Close your eyes and remember the same physical sensations throughout your body that you feel when you do the *"12-Minute Pause."* Relax your body from head to toe, just as you do in the exercise. Then envision yourself in your personal place of relaxation and bring to mind an exam on which you did well.

Try to remember all of the details. How did you feel during the exam? Remember how easily you answered the questions and your sense of satisfaction afterwards?

After you envision this exam and feel the success that you experienced before, say to yourself, "Yes, I can do it. I'll do well on this exam, too!"

Relaxation Enhances Self-Confidence

In a state of relaxation, we have better control over our body's physiological reactions, over our thoughts, and over our emotions. We improve our ability to cope with stressful situations and increase our power of concentration. All of these factors contribute to a greater sense of self-confidence. To strengthen your self-confidence, you can replay, just as in a movie, the positive things that happened to you during the day.

We suggest you do this before going to sleep:

Try to remember your successes more than your failures. Every person has an area in which he or she does well. Recreate the successful moments of the day and the sense of confidence you felt then. Every time you create a feeling of self-confidence, you're reinforcing this conviction.

Here's an exercise for enhancing your self-confidence.

Exercise for Enhancing Self-Confidence

Enter the state of relaxation by yourself. Close your eyes and remember the same physical sensations throughout your body that you feel when you do the *"12-Minute Pause."* Relax your body from head to toe.

Now envision yourself in your personal place. Think of a situation in which you felt full of self-confidence. Recreate that situation as if it were happening again at this very moment.

Recall where you were and what you did when you had that strong feeling of self-confidence.

Notice how you hold your head up high and your body language conveys self-confidence. Say out loud, "Yes, I can!" and smile to yourself. Do this exercise several times until you feel that every time you smile and say, "Yes, I can!" your self-confidence immediately improves.

Relaxation Reduces Fears - How to Overcome the Fear of Flying.

This section is dedicated to Asencion, our friend from Spain who has not yet had a need to fly but wishes to do so, and to the many thousands of people who must fly but who fear to board a plane, and to those for whom just thinking about flying is frightening.

An airport is a place that elicits positive feelings in many people. The airport symbolizes change from the every day routine. The special atmosphere of crowds of people with suitcases who will travel all over the world, is a stimulus to the mind. A visit to the duty-free shops make you feel as if you are already abroad.

Many people, however, are not able to enjoy their visit to the airport. They become nervous and anxious by the mere thought of flying. Studies show that tension and negative expectation may be a cause of heart attacks. New research presented at a cardiologist's convention in Stockholm demonstrated that while waiting at the airport or while flying, the chances of having a heart attack are four times greater than under regular circumstances.

Many people suffer from a fear of flying because in their minds, flying is linked to disasters. They feed their minds with negative images such as that of an airplane crash. They may also think that human beings are not made to fly (although airplanes do fly). They may even say "I read that many pilots drink alcoholic beverages. What happens if a pilot gets drunk?" "What would happen if the engines failed while the plane was flying over the ocean?" "What happens if...?" All these endless questions reinforce their fears.

Is this fear realistic? After all, the fear of flying is disproportional to the actual risks associated with airplanes. Airplanes, are universally considered a safer means of transportation than automobiles. Thus the fear of flying is largely due to runaway imagination. Since it is possible to control our minds, we can overcome the fear of flying.

Fear is a negative expectation about the future. We expect ahead of time that a result will be negative, even if there is very little chance that it will actually turn out that way. In order to change this negative expectation people deny their fear, but this does not help them. Instead of denial, one should concentrate on the positive options by replacing negative expectations with positive ones, preferably while in a state of relaxation.

While relaxed, we imagine what a successful outcome will be - whether we are dealing with flying, selling a house, undergoing a surgical operation, lecturing to an audience, or any other activity which may cause us to feel fear. We have to mentally replace any picture that encourages our fear with other pictures that help us overcome this feeling.

We have to imagine the positive aspects and the favorable outcomes in order to feel as though these results have already been achieved. By concentrating on positive pictures again and again, we increase the chances of making them a reality.

An easy and efficient way to change the images that cause fear is using the Silva Method's "Mirror of the Mind" technique.

Mr. Genaro Aquino, a Silva Method Director in Manhattan, told us about one of his students who had a fear of flying. Prof. Margarita S. feared boarding a plane, and used to take medication which was not of much help. She used the "Mirror of the Mind" technique for one month and was able to solve her problem. She states: "It was the first time in my life that I flew relaxed without any need for pills. I felt strong enough to sit near the window and watch the scenery below me."

We now present the "Mirror of the Mind" technique of the Silva Method. It was adapted to treat the fear of flying.

Exercise for Overcoming the Fear of Flying

After practicing the *"12-Minute Pause"* close your eyes and relax your body from head to toe, as you have done in the recorded exercise. Do it quickly, within a few minutes. Afterwards, envision yourself in your personal place.

Imagine a mirror with a blue frame in front of you. Imagine that you can see a movie playing inside the mirror. There are people boarding an airplane. They are very relaxed, and smiling. You picture an image of yourself slowly joining the crowd in this movie. This image boards the plane despite the fact that its heart is beating rapidly and its hands are sweaty.

Mentally erase this picture from your mirror, and move the mirror from the center of your mental screen to the left. Change the blue colored frame into a white one. Imagine again that an image of yourself is boarding the plane. You may remind the image to relax and alter its feelings. You will make the image feel more relaxed while boarding the plane. Breathing is normal. There is a feeling of safety and security. Thoughts arise about the purpose of the flight – a vacation, a business trip, or a meeting with a loved one.

The image knows that airplanes increase one's chances of communicating with the entire world. Flying enables us to reach our destinations in a few hours. The image observes itself on the plane, feeling calm, controlling its thoughts. The airplane takes off and the image feels relaxed, imagining that in a few

minutes there will be an enjoyable in-flight movie, tasty food, and conversation with a fellow passenger. Then you will imagine the image performing the *"12-Minute Pause."* Your image is now so relaxed that it falls asleep.

During the landing the image trusts the experienced pilot and the expertise of the air control crew, who will ensure a safe landing. The airplane is seen landing, reaching its destination safely.

Congratulate your inner self for changing its feelings and attitude towards flying.

Repeat this exercise a few times, whenever you need it.

Concentrate on the blue-framed mirror, where you visualize the fear, only the first time. Afterwards, concentrate only on the white-framed mental mirror that shows a calm and relaxed image of yourself. Make sure that the feelings of relaxation, safety and happiness of your inner self in the movie become your own feelings.

Relaxation Helps Eliminate Unwanted Habits

Different people react to stress differently: Some smoke, some overeat, and some eat less than their bodies require. Others drink alcohol to excess and still others use drugs.

All of these patterns of behavior that are designed to release the individual from stress ultimately increase it. Look, for example, at overeating. This habit causes weight gain. Our culture frowns on fat people and, in some instances, fat people find it hard to be accepted (they have a harder time getting a job, for example). This situation naturally increases tension.

It's a vicious circle: Under stress, someone may eat more and gain weight, in turn causing more stress and increasing the desire to eat even more to release the tension. The result is weight gain.

The solution: Release the tension that's causing the problem. Knowing how to achieve relaxation gives you more control over your habits and helps you find more suitable solutions to your problems.

After doing the *"12-Minute Pause,"* several times, you'll be able to achieve relaxation on your own and change your habits. Here are two exercises you can do: one for achieving your desired weight and the other for quitting smoking.

Achieving your Desired Weight

After practicing the *"12-Minute Pause,"* you can achieve relaxation on your own. Close your eyes and relax your body from head to toe, just as you do in the recorded exercise. Do this quickly, within a few moments. Then imagine yourself in your personal place.

Imagine yourself facing a large mirror. Your whole body is reflected in front of you, top to bottom.

You observe your thin face, your slender arms, your narrow thighs, flat belly, and shapely legs. Talk to the various parts of your body. Tell them how good they look. Imagine your slim body in the street, at work, at a party, at the pool, together with someone you're interested in.

Feel yourself light, lively, and happy to be thin. Try imagining how a thin person thinks and behaves. You can be just like that. Choosing to be slim gives you a feeling of control. Enjoy it and tell yourself, "What a wonderful sense of control I have when I eat only the desired amount of healthy food."

How to Quit or Cut Down Smoking

If you're a habitual smoker, you can also develop a new habit in your inner consciousness: waiting 5 minutes before lighting a cigarette.

Exercise to Quit Smoking

Every time you feel like smoking, close your eyes and enter a state of relaxation by recalling the pleasant sensations you feel while doing the recorded exercise. Say to yourself: I want to stop smoking and I'm willing to wait 5 minutes before lighting my cigarette. Count up to 3 and open your eyes.

Look at your watch and put the cigarettes somewhere far away from yourself. Occupy yourself with something else (a phone call, reading, watching TV, etc.).

Don't sit and wait or watch the clock until 5 minutes have passed! If you occupy yourself in a natural manner for 5 minutes, you are more than likely to forget the cigarette and remember it only after 15 minutes or half an hour. And then, even if you do eventually smoke, you'll have "gained" an extra half-hour without a cigarette. The time intervals between cigarettes can thus be increased and, as a result, the desire to smoke will arise less frequently, leading to a feeling of control and greater self-esteem.

To eliminate the automatic nature of the smoking habit do the following: When you smoke, cease all other activity. Don't pay attention to anything else except for the cigarette. Don't read, don't drink coffee, and don't speak with others. Devote all of your attention to the act of smoking, so that you are conscious of it. Remember that a habit is something done unconsciously and automatically, while the conscious mind is occupied elsewhere. Making smoking a conscious habit will help you smoke less.

Relaxation Improves Sexual Functioning

Imagination plays a key role in sexual desire. Sexual desire is brought forth through mental images that generate excitement and pleasure. The feelings evoked during sexual activity itself reinforce the desire.

There are people who are afraid of failing in sexual activity. These fears conjure up mental pictures of non-functioning which increase fear and insecurity and impair sexual activity.

Mental images bring about reactions in the body. Someone who is fearful creates unsuitable images that foster further failure. In a state of relaxation, the imagination can be controlled to create ideal experiences of desire and pleasure. These images generate the appropriate reactions in the body that permit the enjoyment of sexual relations in reality.

Exercise to Enjoy Sexual Relations

After practicing the *"12-Minute Pause,"* use your imagination to help improve your sexual functioning. Close your eyes

and relax your body from head to toe, just as you do in the recorded exercise. Do this quickly, within a few minutes. Afterwards, envision yourself in your personal place.

Imagine and recreate the most successful sexual experience you have ever had, saw, read, or imagined. Recreate all of the details and every sensation that you felt.
Bring to mind the caresses, the kisses, and the warm touch of your skin on the body of your partner.
Feel how these images increase your level of desire without fear or anxiety, and how you feel confident enough to allow your body to experience pleasure.

Relaxation Raises the Level of Creativity

Creativity enables us to solve problems in new and innovative ways. When we're in a state of relaxation, our inner consciousness operates under greater freedom, without the tough and limiting control of our conscious mind. This state allows new and creative ideas to rise to consciousness.

Newton, for example, was reclining under a fruit tree when he discovered the principle of gravity. Archimedes discovered the principle that bears his name while blissfully taking a bath. Einstein thought up the theory of relativity while lying in bed and resting after an illness.

In a state of calmness, our inner consciousness is capable of reorganizing information at our disposal, thereby creating new ideas and finding solutions that were not previously imagined.

Our level of creativity increases in a state of relaxation because we're more open to mental images that facilitate new ideas. You can take advantage of this creativity in any field of interest for you: work, interpersonal relations, a technical or artistic project.

To raise your level of creativity we suggest the following exercise:

Exercise for Stimulating Creative Ideas

After practicing the *"12-Minute Pause,"* close your eyes and relax your body from head to toe, just as you do in the recorded exercise. Do it quickly, within a few minutes. Afterwards, envision yourself in your personal place.

Imagine yourself watching a movie screen. Think of the subject in which you want a new idea. Remain relaxed and full of faith and the expectation that you'll indeed come up with it. The creative idea will appear on the screen during the exercise, or it will float into your brain during the course of the day.

Relaxation Increases Self-Awareness

Are you aware of the fact that our minds are constantly occupied with thinking about what has already happened or what could happen in the future? What happened to me this morning? What will happen tomorrow? We almost never take a look at the "here and now," and we are rarely aware of what's happening to us at this very second in our body and mind.

One Yogi used to say, "The problem with you westerners is that you're never at home!"

He was, of course, referring to the "here and now," to a situation in which we are aware of the present moment.

During relaxation we are more aware of our body, our thoughts, our emotions, and our desires. As a result, we are more in touch with our inner consciousness. When you enter a state of relaxation, you absorb information that did not rise to your consciousness under normal circumstances, and you are able to transmit desired messages to your inner consciousness. You are therefore more in touch with yourself, more aware of your skills, your desires, and your real needs. At this stage there is greater compatibility between your inner world and your outer world functioning.

One special way to retrieve information from your inner consciousness is through a pendulum. In the section "Relaxation Has a Beneficial Effect on Emotions and Thoughts," you used a pendulum to prove the effect of the imagination on the body. Now we'll explain how to use a pendulum to enable communication between the conscious mind and the inner consciousness.

Your inner consciousness contains a great deal of information that does not always reach you when you are aware. You can ask your inner consciousness questions regarding any subject of interest, and then get answers from it. Sample questions you might ask are whether or not you're compatible with someone (a new romantic interest, a business partner, someone to share an apartment with); which profession to choose (whether you have the suitable skills); the right place for you to work ; how to find an object that was lost, etc.

The pendulum is not a magical device. Using it is a way to obtain answers from your inner consciousness by way of your muscle movements.

In order to permit the muscle movements to be felt you must hold the pendulum in a certain way and set up a code that will enable you to receive and understand the messages that your inner consciousness sends you through the pendulum.

On a table, place the piece of paper with the two intersecting lines that you prepared earlier, a horizontal and a vertical one.

Sit comfortably, and rest your elbow on the table just as before. Hold the end of the pendulum between your two fingers above the intersection of the two lines. Close your eyes and ask the pendulum in which direction it moves when the answer is "yes." Wait a few seconds and open your eyes. Notice in which direction the pendulum is swaying. This direction symbolizes "yes."

Now close your eyes and ask the pendulum which direction it moves when the answer is "no." Wait a few seconds, open your eyes, and notice which direction the pendulum is moving. This direction means "no."

It is possible that your inner consciousness does not have the information you want, or that it would be better if this information did not reach you. Allow the pendulum to protect you from this information. Close your eyes again and ask the pendulum in which direction it moves to indicate "I don't know." or "I don't want to tell you." Wait a few seconds and open your eyes. Notice in which direction the pendulum is swaying. In this case the inner consciousness refuses to inform the conscious mind. Let's asume that our inner consciousness has always a good reason and a positive intention, even when it withholds information.

To make sure you're getting correct answers, it's important that you be relaxed, at ease, and focused. The more you're in control of your thoughts and feelings through relaxation exercises, the more the answers that you get from your inner consciousness, will be correct.

5
A Positive Approach and Success

A Positive Approach and Success

It has been shown that successful people were mentally convinced they were going to succeed before they actually achieved success.

What distinguishes one person from another is the nature of the dialogue that the person carries on internally. If this dialogue is negative, a person tends to be anxious and depressed. If the dialogue is positive, however, it enables the person to transform obstacles into a force that motivates him or her to advance toward goals.

"You are what you think you are" expresses the idea that our thoughts determine who we are. Dr. Emile Coue made use of this concept at the beginning of the century. He asked his patients to repeat the following sentence several times a day: "Day by day, in every way, I am getting better and better." Surprisingly, the health of many of these patients improved significantly, and some of them even recovered completely. The positive statement influences not just mood, but health itself.

For a period of more than twenty years, Napoleon Hill, author of *"Think and Grow Rich,"* interviewed and researched the most financially successful people of his generation. Hill discovered that the secret to their success was their way of thinking. They used positive thinking.

Positive thinking begins with an optimistic approach that looks at the positive side of every event and situation. Someone with positive thinking has faith in his or her ability to realize desires or aspirations, and a belief that one can have an impact on events and their final outcome.

This individual is able to see the incremental steps of progress, even if the end result has not yet been achieved. He or she develops an expectation to have the desired results materialize, and thus steers behavior in the direction of success.

Life deals us both happy and sad moments. The way we experience these moments depends on ourselves alone. "We'll give thanks for the laughter and the tears," says Argentinean singer Mercedes Sosa in her famous song *"Gracias a la Vida"* [Thank You, Life]. This is the outlook of successful people.

To succeed, we must develop a positive approach. It's easy to be positive when everything is going well. It's less easy to think positively when work is going poorly, when your closest relationship is coming apart at the seams, or when the children are ill. But despite it all, a positive approach must be maintained in order to succeed. Developing a positive approach takes time, but it can be accomplished by consistent and determined effort.

How does one succeed? Like a computer, our brain absorbs information from the world and from people around us. Based upon the information in this data bank we decide who we are, what we are capable of doing, and what is beyond our capabilities. When you feed this personal computer (your brain) with negative data in the form of negative thoughts – hatred, jealousy, frustration, or fear – you block the entry of positive data. Therefore, in a state of depression you'll remember only your failures and unpleasant experiences, concluding that this is how it will always be because in this situation, only negative experiences are evoked from memory.

On the other hand, positive data that we have also fed into our brain enabled us to be what we are today, encompassing all the skills we have developed and the successes we have had in the personal, social, and material realms.

If you, like most people, find it easier to recall the negative data, this is a sign that you haven't used your brain sufficiently to reinforce your positive experiences. You may decide to think positively and even manage to pull it off for several hours, until you ultimately return to your more typical behavior.

However, if you faithfully practice relaxation with The *"12-Minute Pause,"* it will be easier for you to take a positive approach. This is because in a state of relaxation you can influence your inner consciousness (previously known as the subconscious), thereby bringing about an internal change of behavior.

Self Esteem and the Programming of Goals

Self-esteem is the relationship we have with ourselves; it is how much we appreciate and value ourselves.

Self-esteem manifests itself in different areas of our lives. We see it in the importance we place on our personal capacities at work, with the family and in social relationships. In each of the fields we have different values for ourselves that do not always correspond with reality. In the majority of cases we undervalue ourselves. We do not know our own talents and hence we do not use them. We cannot be successful in any area in which we have low self-esteem.

The lack of self-esteem limits people, and makes any problem that presents itself even worse. When someone thinks: "I don't have the capacity to get a job," or "without a doubt I will fail," or "this was not meant for me," all of these internal dialogues limit one's self and do not permit the person to use the capacities that s/he possesses. The lack of self-esteem and the lack of success stories are inextricably linked.

Self-esteem is built from past successes. Failures help us learn, but only successes can serve as reference points that are essential for future successes.

How do we reach success so as to accomplish what we desire? First, we must know what it is that we desire, and what our goals are.

The problem with many people is that they do not have well-defined goals, they do not know what it is that they want. They have dreams, fantasies of accomplishing something by mere fate of luck. Luck, however, follows those who actively search it, those who do something to convert their dreams into reality.

The first step is to have a predetermined goal. For some it might be important to recuperate their health, or to make more money; others are in search of an affectionately-gratifying relationship (with their partners, children). There are other people who want to triumph in the arts, at work, in business, politics, or sports. Others just want positive changes in their personalities: greater maturity, or to be better friends, better parents, and better people actively contributing to the society in which they live.

The more defined and clearer the goals we have, and the greater the detail of our imagined plans, the stronger the desire will be. These goals will also help to stimulate our minds. We need to believe that the goal we are proposing to ourselves is within our reach. This does not mean that it will be easy to achieve, but that it is possible and appropiate to our abilities and our personalities.

Once we know what our goal is, we must picture it in our minds as if it were already a reality. We must imagine its every detail, and make this image as clear, strong and persistent as possible, in order for it to grab hold of our conscience. As long as we keep this image of our goal in mind we are being directed toward it, and we are actively seeking it.

After all, the way in which a person behaves is the result of what s/he thinks and visualizes. Once we act upon our goal, we will immediately have a response of some sort, which will enable us to evaluate the effectiveness of our efforts. We will observe if our actions are bringing us closer to our goals, or whether we should make some changes to be successful.

How much we want from life has a price in terms of money, effort, planning and studies. Everything is possible, even if some of our living conditions might make us think otherwise. When we think that it is impossible to overcome an illness, surpass poverty, find a partner, or be successful anywhere, we are creating our reality from these negative thoughts.

If we change our thoughts we can create those things which we desire. All that is needed is an intense desire as well as constantly imagining our successes. This drive will lead us toward the necessary steps that are indispensable for this success. It is not simple to maintain a continuous string of successful thoughts when circumstances are difficult. The rewards of doing so, however, are great.

When we can direct our thoughts we can change our circumstances. Our mind can stimulate the body's healing resources in order to cure itself, as well as create ideas that can make the needed money for us. Understanding this truth will bring success in any endeavor.

The Conscious Mind and Inner Consciousness

Our brain operates on two different levels The conscious mind is the rational part that observes and thinks, and the inner consciousness (or subconscious) includes everything that is not in the conscious mind at a given moment. All our experiences and life events influence both the conscious mind and the inner consciousness.

Our inner consciousness is responsible for most of the learning we do during our lifetime. It does what it was "programmed" to do even before we were born, and adds to this the commands of the conscious mind, for better or worse. All our habits and patterns of behavior result from a process of learning that was either conscious or unconscious. These habits and behaviors become automatic. For example, we're capable of fluent speech without having to think about every word. When we learn a foreign language, however, we think about each word, which interrupts the flow.

When playing tennis, an athlete does not think about each and every movement – where to run, how to turn the racket, etc. These movements come automatically.

What would it be like if a pianist had to guide the muscles of each finger in order to play? The result would be less than harmonious.

How did we learn how to drive? At first, we had to think about every movement - how to change gears, brake, accelerate. After we learned, driving became more and more automatic.

Behavior patterns also become automatic. This is true not only for patterns that are positive, but also for those we are less happy about – shyness, impulsiveness, jealousy, and lack of confidence, for example. These patterns do not change through efforts of the conscious mind because the automatic reaction, which requires no effort, is much stronger.

Therefore, without cooperation from the inner consciousness, none of our efforts will be worth anything. We all know people who gain weight back after a successful diet, or who take up smoking again after having quit, or who continue to be aggressive despite their promises to the contrary.

When this happens, it means that the inner consciousness was not partner to the decision to lose weight, quit smoking, or change behavior patterns.

We have to persuade our inner consciousness to participate, and that's easier to do in a state of relaxation. Relaxation is the ideal state for influencing the inner consciousness. In a state of calm, the inner consciousness willingly accepts the suggestions of the conscious mind, and is capable of changing those thoughts and beliefs that do not help us attain our goals.

For example, if we are afraid, rational thought may help, but it's not enough to overcome the fear. In a state of relaxation, we can exchange the old program recorded in our inner consciousness for a new program that helps us overcome the fear, because the inner consciousness accepts it.

When we transmit new information to the inner consciousness in a state of relaxation, the new information takes the place of the old information on the same topic. Denial is useless for changing a negative emotion ("I'm not afraid"). It is far more effective to develop an opposing emotion to take its place ("I'm brave").

When we reach the inner consciousness through relaxation, we can influence it to forget what is hindering us and we can learn the things that we choose to learn.

The suggestions that we propose for reaching the inner consciousness are given in the form of positive statements. These will be accepted if they seem reasonable. The positive statements are accompanied by corresponding mental images. Mental images are the best tool for reaching the inner consciousness. All of us imagine things, but few of us use imagination in a deliberate and controlled manner purposely for our own benefit.

How can we make effective use of the imagination? When we think of a positive statement, we can envision it in our mind's eye written in large shiny letters. We can imagine someone repeating the statement over and over again.

We can also imagine the contents of the statement and envision that the goal we are aiming for has already been achieved. For example, if you think your memory is poor and wish to improve it, you can repeat statement number 13 to yourself: "I have an excellent memory; I'm calm, alert, and can absorb any information that I wish to remember."

How can you imagine this statement in your mind's eye? In a state of relaxation, you're calm and able to pay attention to the subject you wish to remember. You envision yourself saying to one of your friends that you're able to recall things in great detail and that your memory is improving from day to day.

Your inner consciousness will receive the new program: "My memory is excellent." Being relaxed is the ideal state for changing the programs recorded in your inner consciousness. Some people find it hard to see with their mind's eye. When we are relaxed and the brain is producing alpha waves, our ability to see with our mind's eye and to use mental images improves.

It is not necessary for the images to be clear and detailed. Seeing them vaguely is good enough, as long as they can be identified. You certainly feel different when you imagine yourself with a stranger than you do when you imagine you are with someone you love. Even if you don't picture them clearly in your mind's eye, you definitely know the difference between them.

Positive Statements

Because of the fact that our inner consciousness was programmed over a long period of time (and not always consciously), every attempt to change these programs or to introduce new ones must be carried out under the following conditions:

1. A state of relaxation

The programming must be done while relaxed. Relaxation helps us overcome fears and negative beliefs (for example, that we cannot attain good health, love, business success, etc.). In a state of relaxation, we think positively, because, as noted earlier, it's impossible to feel anxiety, fear, or other negative emotions when our muscles are fully relaxed.

2. Formulating the positive statement

Suitable positive statements must follow three rules:

a. The statement must be brief so that it can be easily memorized.

b. The statement must be worded in the present tense, so that it can be turned into a concrete reality. For example, "I am succeeding" rather than "I will succeed."

c. Avoid negative words or mentioning what you're trying to eliminate. For example, instead of saying "I'm not afraid" say "I'm brave;" instead of "I'm not sick" say "I'm healthy." The object is to refrain from mental images of fear or illness and to reinforce positive images.

If we say to a little child, "Don't break the cup," he just might break it because he has already seen it broken in his mind's eye. It's better to tell him, "Pick up the cup carefully."

3. Repeating the positive statement

We must repeat the positive statement in order to instill it into our inner consciousness. Repetition is the basis of all our habits and skills.

The more we repeat the positive statement when fully relaxed, the more the inner consciousness accepts it and turns it into reality.

Here are some examples of positive statements:

1. *Health:* I'm healthy: my body is strong and full of energy.

2. *Serenity:* I'm calm in every situation.

3. *Concentration:* I concentrate on any subject at will.

4. *Relaxation:* I attain good relaxation whenever I wish.

5. *Self-discipline:* I make a decision and stick to it.

6. *Efficiency:* I work in a systematic and organized manner.

7. *Perseverance:* I keep trying until I succeed.

8. *Enthusiasm:* I'm full of enthusiasm and joie-de-vivre, and I radiate this onto others.

9. *Maturity:* I weigh and judge matters before I react.

10. *Communication:* I develop good relationships with my family, my friends, and my work colleagues.

11. *Self-confidence:* I'm self-confident in every situation.

12. *Success:* I succeed in all my objectives.

13. *Memory:* I have an excellent memory. I'm calm, alert, and absorb any information that I wish to remember.

14. **Energy:** My level of energy is very high and helps me enjoy life to the fullest.

15. **Creativity:** I think of new and original ways to solve problems and they work.

16. **Public speaking:** I express myself with confidence and create a good rapport with my audience.

17. **Understanding:** I have good insight into the people around me, and I know how to help them in different situations.

18. **Ambitions:** I have goals in life, and I act accordingly to achieve them.

19. **Aggressiveness:** I cope with frustration in an assertive manner.

20. **Optimism:** I have a positive outlook and fully expect to succeed.

Do these statements speak to you? We each have our own preferences. What is important to one person may be insignificant to another. You must create your own positive statements based upon your needs, beliefs, and personality.

Think of statements flowing with personal meaning that can help and encourage you. These will be powerful statements. Repeating them in a state of relaxation will instill them in your inner consciousness, which will accept them and enable you to attain your goal.

We suggest that you adapt the positive statement according to what you believe is possible and what you desire to accomplish, and engage your inner consciousness in a dialogue to persuade it to agree to your request.

6
Teaching Children Relaxation and Positive Thinking

CHAPTER 6

Teaching Children Relaxation and Positive Thinking

Parents who regularly address their children in a positive manner are helping them develop.

Parents who want to prepare their children for success in life must teach them how to relax and think positively. These factors affect our character, our approach, and our behavior.

Relaxation

Children should be taught relaxation from an early age, before they acquire negative habits of tightening their muscles and other exaggerated responses to stress. Through relaxation, parents can teach their children to cope with stress. This tool will serve them well all their lives.

A good way to teach children relaxation is by doing the *"12-Minute Pause"* with them until they can do it alone. The entire family can do the exercise together whenever possible. Children learn by imitation. If they see their parents doing a relaxation exercise, that's the best incentive for them to also want to learn relaxation.

A graduate of the Silva course did her relaxation exercises everyday. When her son was two and a half years old, he asked what she was doing and she explained that this was an exercise to feel well and do better at work.

One day, she came upon her son sitting at ease on the couch with his eyes closed. She asked him what he was doing, and the boy replied, "An exercise so that when I go to nursery school, the children and the teacher will be able to understand me."

The boy had a speech impediment that made it difficult for anyone other than his parents to understand him. Before he was to begin nursery school, his mother tried to coach him to speak more clearly. She said that speaking clearly was important so that the teacher and children would understand him. The boy had certainly found a good role model for solving his problems.

Relaxation exercises should become a habit, like brushing one's teeth. As relaxation becomes a part of their lives, children will become calmer and better able to cope with demands made on them.

Positive Thinking

If we teach our children to think positively, we encourage them to use all the skills at their command to accomplish their goals. The results will be visible in their daily approach to life and greater happiness. Children raised in this way will grow up to be what they believe about themselves. If a child believes that he or she will succeed, success in the outer world will be a natural extension of that belief.

Children have a natural optimism to some degree, but education has an important role to play: One can choose to think in a positive manner. A child's thoughts do not appear randomly, but are the product of what the child absorbs from his or her surroundings. Children are often subject to heavy criticism and very little praise. If a child constantly hears criticism and blame, he or she learns to feel worthless and loses confidence. If, on the other hand, he hears encouragement and love, the child learns to love himself.

Parents who regularly address their children in a positive manner are helping them develop. We're capable of even changing our feelings by what we say to our children. Therefore, positive statements have considerable power and influence.

There are moments when children are more open to suggestion, such as just before they fall asleep. This is an ideal time to tell our children that we love them very much. When children get this positive message before falling asleep, their sleep will be more peaceful and refreshing. The message will reinforce their physical and emotional defenses, and will better protect them against infection, and their learning and disposition will improve. Frequent repetition of the positive statements will bring about impressive results.

Bloch and Merritt (1995) suggest that positive statements be used with children to convey unconditional love that is not contingent upon their behavior. Some examples:

I love you just the way you are.
I'm fond of you.
There's no one quite like you.
God smiled when you were born.

How do we teach children to create their own positive statements? Ask them which of their qualities, skills, or achievements they like, and repeat together, over, and over, the statement you create.

For example:
I'm smart and happy.
I'm a good boy/girl and I like myself.
I'm a great athlete in school.

Children can create positive statements to overcome fear, to improve their self-esteem or confidence, or to achieve a specific objective. It's easy to create positive statements and use them.

Positive statements must have three qualities
They should be expressed in the first person.
They should be made in the present tense.
They should be worded positively.

Examples of statements against fear:

I'm calm and I'm thinking of something pleasant.
I'm calm and I'm thinking of a happy song.
My parents are protecting me.
I have power and can defend myself or ask for help.

Examples of statements to enhance self esteem:

I'm smart.
I like myself.
I have lots of friends.
I'm capable of doing lots of things. (Mention the child's special talents – drawing, singing, acting, studying, self-expression, laughing, helping others.)

Examples of statements for specific objectives:

Objective: To pass an exam
Statements:
I prepared well for the exam.
I remember other exams that I did well in. I'll do well this time, too.

Objective: To make friends
Statements:
It's easy for me to make good friends.
Other kids like me and enjoy my friendship.

Objective: To do well in sports
Statements:
I'm a good football player.
I practice and do better all the time.

All positive statements are reinforced by repetition and become part of the child. Children can recite to themselves the appropriate positive statements whenever needed, during relaxation or even during the course of their regular activities. They can say the statements out loud or silently.

To teach your children to appreciate and enjoy the positive things in life, read them the poems of Adula, written especially for this book. We suggest you read these poems before sleep or during storytelling hour, although they can also be read at other hours of the day.

Poems by Adula

Seeing

Look at the sea, a deep, dark blue,
So deeply blue meant just for you!
Now see the sky, a cloud, the sun,
The rainbow when the rain is done!
Look at the tree, an emerald green!
How lucky that it can be seen –

Though some don't see at all.

A soft white cloud, a pretty tree,
And you can see, yes, you can see!
Don't pity those who can't,
But you
Are rich with sight
The gift of day and night!

Think of the sea, the perfect blue,
The yellow sand that's fun for you,
See the sky, the tree, the cloud
And say a thank you out loud,

For you
Can see them too!

Hearing

Listen to the roar of the sea
Alive with power and mystery!

Hear the water trickling past
In streams and rivers, slow and fast.

Listen to the rain fall on leaves,
Drip, drip, drop, on hat and sleeves,

Hear the chirping of the birds,
The songs they sing are just like words,

Hear the voice of your best chum,
Cheer up, my dear, and don't be glum.

The world has such a beautiful sound
Listen well, it's all around,

The music of life, precious and dear
Sounds that not everyone can hear.

Talking

You can share the way you feel,
Say the words your lips unseal,
Shout with joy or make amends,
Talk with Mom and Dad or friends,

You can whisper or sing full voice,
Loud or soft – you have a choice.
The sounds you make are very dear,
Not everyone can speak or hear.

Height

Not tall as a flag?
Not a basketball star?
Football's fun, too,
And will get you quite far.

Not handsome or pretty?
Too thin or too fat?
What counts is your brain
And one day everyone
Will see that!

Asking

Today will soon be gone,
Never to come back.
Consider what you have,
And ask for what you lack.

If you do not ask,
Time will slip away;
Think of what you want,
And say the words today!

Discuss these poems with your children. Draw their attention to all the treasures they possess. They can see, hear, speak. Ask them how they use all these senses for their enjoyment:

What do they do that makes them happy?
What words or pleasant music do they like to hear?
What do they like to talk about?
What talents do they have and how would they like to develop them?
Teach them to fill their minds with positive thoughts and encourage them to see themselves as independent, happy, and very much loved.

7
How Teachers Can Help
Their Students

CHAPTER 7

How Teachers Can Help Their Students

In a positive, optimistic atmosphere, teaching and learning become more enjoyable and more interesting for all.

The simple tools we present here will help teachers to help their students learn more successfully and to enjoy themselves while doing it. Teaching children relaxation techniques strengthens their self-confidence and helps them to set and achieve goals. The few uncomplicated, highly effective skills illustrated below will positively influence children's development and enable each individual child to make better progress in school and in other aspects of his or her life.

In order to facilitate the teaching of relaxation in the classroom, we are pleased to present classroom teachers with a brief exercise based on the *"12-Minute Pause."*

Brief Exercise for Students

Sit comfortably and close your eyes.
In this exercise, we'll work our way down from head to toe and reach physical relaxation.

Turn your attention inward. We aware of the different parts of your face. Notice your forehead... let it be smooth and relaxed. Release the muscles that express worry, let your brow become entirely smooth.

Your eyes are lightly closed, without wrinkling your brow. You can feel the air entering and leaving like a gentle, soft wave,

and as you deepen your relaxation, your breath becomes slower, more regular, deeper.

Turn your attention to your back. Feel your back loosen and relax, more and more.

Turn your attention to your abdomen. Feel your abdomen loosen, relax, and soften. Let your breath pass through it. Feel the muscles of your hips loosen and relax. Relax your thighs and knees. Relax your feet.
Now your entire body is soft and relaxed. You have already reached physical relaxation.

To reach mental relaxation here's some help in seeing and feeling peaceful scenes.

Imagine yourself walking in a forest on a beautiful day. There's a pleasant breeze. The sun is peeking through the trees, its yellow rays in a play of light and shadow. You enjoy the warmth and continue to walk. Your eyes notice flowers in a profusion of colors, a carpet of color between the trees.
Look at the flowers. Notice their colors. Inhale the fragrance into your lungs.

You hear a fluttering of wings. You look up and glimpse a flock of birds. Two birds land not far from your path and begin to peck eagerly at the ground.
Your ears notice their happy chirping. You feel serenity and peace.

You are in a state of deeper relaxation than before.
Now imagine yourself in your personal place, a place that's

pleasurable for you.
You are already in your personal place and enjoying it. (Wait
for a half a minute)

You are in a state of deeper relaxation than before. The more
you repeat this exercise, the more easily you'll reach physical
and mental relaxation, and enjoy the positive effects of the
exercise.

I'll count from one to three. At the count of three, open your
eyes and you'll feel refreshed and well.
1- Begin coming out slowly.
2-Notice your hands and move your fingers. Move your feet
and the muscles of your face. Open and close your hands. Feel
the energy flowing in your body.
3- Let your eyes open. You are alert and feel well.

Guided by the teacher, students who learn this important relaxation
technique improve their concentration and increase their chances
for academic and personal achievement!
For teachers, this is another valuable tool to help students be more
relaxed and focused in real-life situations. Practicing relaxation
will result in an overall improvement characterized by:

Positive thinking
Increased self-confidence
Better test-taking abilities
Higher scholastic achievement
More appropriate personal and social relationships

Following are the accounts of two Silva Method instructors who
explain how the Method can benefit school children.

Rivka Cohen

"It has been my good fortune to be both a teacher of the Silva Method and a teacher of young children. I was able to use the knowledge gained from the Silva Method to impart to children some tools to help them successfully cope with the different challenges in their lives. The children completely assimilated the real meaning of positive thinking and learned to use it.

"In one of my classes, the school nurse came in and announced to the children that there would be immunization shots given the following week. The children were told to bring in their health records.

Naturally, the children were less than enthusiastic about the idea and they systematically "forgot" to bring in their health cards, hoping they could avoid getting the shots. They were also very tense. Every knock on the classroom door made them jump. I felt their distress and I asked them where it was easier to inject a needle, into a pillow or a wooden desk. The answer was obvious. I told them that if they relaxed the muscles in their arms, making it as soft and pliable as a pillow, the needle would go in easily and wouldn't hurt.

"We did exercises to feel the difference between a tensed arm and a relaxed one. The children visualized themselves getting the shots with a smile, feeling no pain from the needle.
We practiced this brief exercise for the next few days. The day of reckoning arrived. The school nurse came into the classroom, armed with her needles, ready for the usual tension in such cases. To her surprise, the children greeted her with smiling, happy faces.

"It took a moment for one of the children to volunteer to be first, but after that, with joking and kidding around and even some laughter, all the children got their shots. They held out their arms for the needle, took a deep breath, and imagined themselves relaxed and calm, receiving the injection without pain, while also visualizing themselves involved in an activity they enjoyed.

"The nurse told me that in all her years of work in the schools, this was the very first time that an entire class had received its shots without any resistance or crying whatsoever. She was amazed.

"In order to reinforce their self confidence, the children in my classes learned to repeat positive sentences to themselves. The importance of doing this was easy to explain. I asked them what happens when we think of a food we like. Our mouths water and we are ready to eat it right away. And when we think of something sad, we become sad! If we think of something funny, we laugh. So if when I think of something delicious my mouth begins to water and when I think of something sad I am sad and when I think of something that is funny I laugh, what will happen if I think I am a poor student? Or if I think I will fail in something? I behave accordingly.

"In class, at the start of the school day, we would often practice and refine our positive statements. The children would suggest them and we would make a list on the board.

Some examples:
I am calm and relaxed.
I am a good student.
I get 100% on all my tests.

I have a lot of friends.
I am well-liked.
I feel healthy and strong.

Then, each child would close her/his eyes and practice these sentences, adding others that were especially important to them, such as:

I get along with my brothers and sisters.
I get up dry in the morning.
I straighten up my room.
I enjoy doing my homework.
I'm good in math.

"Many of the children wrote down their sentences on a piece of paper and practiced them at home, usually at bedtime. Some years ago, the Board of Education gave regional exams to evaluate the children's achievements in language and math beginning in the first grade. The teachers were understandably concerned in anticipation of the test results. Their agitation was passed on unconsciously to the students. Before taking these tests (and other, regular ones) I would take the children through a short relaxation exercise to prepare them for success. After such practice, each child perceived of her/himself as calm and relaxed, answering the test questions and getting 100% on the test. The relaxation and preparation helped the children to score better on the tests without unnecessary pressure or tension.

"Several weeks ago I went into a pet shop and was pleasantly surprised to find that the shop owner had once been a pupil of mine. We started talking and I remembered him as a child in the first grade.

"I always placed learning material in my classroom to encourage the children to write and express themselves freely. There were many books, pictures and encyclopedias.

This boy, as a young child, had difficulties in writing. I tried hard to interest him in different book and subject so that he would write. One day I brought an animal encyclopedia into the classroom. This was the book that changed things for him. He loved it and didn't let anyone else touch it for several days. He looked through it over and over and then he began to write. I remember he wrote a report on one of the animals in the book. I was so enthusiastic about his success that I told my colleagues about it, and of course, the boy's parents.

From that time on, the boy's resistance to writing was gone. To my surprise, my former first grade student, now a grown man, clearly remembered the incident, including that he had written about fish. His mother still keeps the report he wrote in first grade. It was a turning point in the boy's life. It is interesting of course to note that today he is the proprietor of a pet shop!

"I loved my work in schools. Every day was filled with new and varied challenges. In any classroom there are children with different levels and kinds of capabilities and talents. Each child is unique, a world unto her/himself.

The real challenge for me was to reach a child who had a particular difficulty. I always took into consideration the fact that that child would someday be an adult whom I might meet on the street. I wanted to meet my former pupils and to look them in the eye, firm in the knowledge that I had done all I could for them- that I had given them my very best.

"At home when I would practice relaxation and was in the alpha state, I would often try to figure out what it was that was bothering a certain child. What could I do to help him? What would I do if the child were mine? When we want to help our own children, our motivation is high and we can sometimes be quite creative. The relaxation exercises helped me to help others, especially those children who had special problems. Every child has good qualities. They simply have to be found and encouraged."

Burt Goldman

In his book *"How to better your life with Mind Control,"* Burt Goldman, a senior instructor of Silva in the United States, told us about Marsha Mark , an Silva instructor for children.

"A girl named Cindy joined one of her childrens' courses. Cindy had the unfortunate experience of being told by her father again and again that she was stupid, and she came to believe that. Marsha wanted to show to the children that there's truly no such thing as a stupid child. So she gave them to read a sheet containing a story of George Washington crossing the Delaware River. It read like this:

> It was Christmas Day, 1776, and snow was gently falling in the forest along the Delaware River.
> General George Washington had under his command 2200 ragtailed troops who would rather have been back on their farms than where they were, shivering in the freezing afternoon cold. Hungry and tired, they waited patiently for the command none of them was anxious to hear.
> "Into the rowboats, men. Let's cross the river and attack."
> On the other side of the Delaware stood a row of cabins. In the cabins were the Hessians, an army hired by the British to fight the revolutionary colonists. These men were the enemy. George Washington's troops attacked the Hessians and the United States was born.

The instructor said to Cindy " We're going to have a test on this page later in the afternoon." Cindy looked up, her eyes opening wide. "My mommy told me we weren't supposed to take any tests in this class."

The teacher responded: "That's correct Cindy. The test is only to show you that you are as smart as anybody in this class."

Then Marsha asked her to read the paper again. She spent a few minutes looking it over and then handed it back.

"All right, Cindy. Now that is the way you normally read. I'm going to show you a new way to read your lessons. I want you to make pictures in your mind while you are reading. I want you to visualize. Let's go over this story again. Let's take this first sentence here: It was Christmas Day, 1776, and snow was falling in the forest along the Delaware River.

"How are you going to make a picture out of that?"

"I don't know," she said.

"All right, let me show you. First of all, it's a forest, isn't it? Close your eyes."

She did so.

" Now, imagine that you are in the forest. You are standing in the forest. Can you see that?"

She said, "No."

Marsha said, "Pretend that you are in a forest."

"Oh, all right."

"Are you in a forest?"

"Yes," was her reply.

"There are trees all around you."

"Yes."

" Make it snow. Is it snowing?"

She said, "Yes."

Then Marsha said, "All right, now it's Christmas. I want you to put a Christmas tree in the forest."

Now she smiled.

"You have the Christmas tree?"

"Yes," she said.

" Put a star on the top of it."

She did so.

"Now there's snow falling. You feel the snow?"

"Yes"

"And it's Christmas, isn't it?"

"Yes. "

"At the edge of the forest there is a little river. Can you see the river.?"

"Yes."

"Now," the teacher said to her, "Have you ever seen a 76 gas station?"

"Oh yes," she said, " they're all over."

"Yes, they are. Now, I want you to see seventeen 76 gas stations. Can you see seventeen of them?"

"All right." She put seventeen 76 gas stations on the far side of the river.

"Cindy, what was the name of the river? Do you know?"

"No," she said.

"It's the Delaware River. With your eyes closed I want you to think of the poem "The Farmer in the Dell.""

"Oh yes, I know that one," she said.

"All right, see the farmer in the dell because that is what that river is – the dell – the Delaware."

She grinned now. "This is fun," she said, still with her eyes closed.

"Now, around George Washington and around you, I want you to see a lot of soldiers. I want you to see twenty-two hundred soldiers. How are you going to see twenty-two hundred soldiers, Cindy?"

Now really getting into the game, she said, " Well, I'm going to put a big 22 on top of two owls."

"Fine, why two owls?"

"Because of the big eyes."

"Well, you can put it under one owl and you have the two zeros for the two owl eyes."

"Oh, yes," she said, and so she put a 22 on the top of a big owl, getting into the game.

And so it went.

Cindy began to realize that she was not a dummy. It was the method which she had been using to put the information into her mind that was wrong. Now she used a different method of processing the information. Her mother reported some months afterward that Cindy went from C's and D's to straight A's. Of course, her mother did work with her, helping her to use the method."

We hope this material and the examples will encourage teachers to use these tools to help their pupils in the classroom and in their everyday lives.

Daily practice of relaxation results in positive relationships among the pupils themselves as well as between pupils and teachers.

In a positive, optimistic atmosphere, teaching and learning become more enjoyable and more interesting for all.

Children who have trouble with subjects such as math or grammar can overcome their difficulties by the practiced use of positive, reinforcing statements.

When children worry that they won't understand or don't have the capacity to learn a certain subject, their fear can create a self-fulfilling prophecy. In contrast, relaxation techniques help them think and feel positive about themselves. Their attitude changes and it is much easier for them to comprehend the material being studied.

To help children set goals, they can be asked, while in a state of relaxation, to visualize the positive results they want to achieve in the coming week. They will picture themselves in appropriate situations, carrying out required activities, attaining their goals.

When students enter a state of relaxation and perceive themselves learning things easily, succeeding and enjoying good relationships with others, better results are attained in every subject. Moreover, the child gains a valuable tool with which to succeed in school and in life.

Fear and anxiety of test taking can be overcome when children are guided through the exercise by their teacher.

When students are afraid, their concentration diminishes and their minds begin to wander. Energy is dissipated. Clarity of perception dwindles, as does memory and the ability to focus.

When relaxed, however, the picture changes: children are optimistic, confident, and better able to concentrate. Recall and memory improve and the solutions to problems flow from the brain. This enables students to gather strength and overcome difficulties, because the exercise inculcates a sense of success directly into the inner consciousness. Of course, students' success is also important to teachers.

Several days before an important examination, the children can review the following relaxation exercise under the teacher's guidance.

Exercise for Improved Perfomance on Examinations
(under the teacher's guidance)

(Teacher: Read the short relaxation exercise. After reading the exercise, continue)

Your heart beat is slow and even. You feel peaceful and happy. Everything you have studied for the test is "filed" inside your mind. Any moment you wish to recall this material, simply open the file and the content will appear in your mind. You are sure of yourself, and you know that you will perform well on the test.
When you hand in your test, you feel proud of your work and you know you have successfully taken the test and passed it.

Now I will count from 1 to 3. At the count of 3 open your eyes. You will be alert, relaxed and full of self-confidence.
1- 2 - 3. Eyes open, you are alert and you feel very good, even better than you felt before the exercise.

8
Relaxation for Pregnancy and Childbirth

CHAPTER 8

Relaxation for Pregnancy and Childbirth

The feelings and thoughts of the
mother have a direct impact
on the baby before it is born.

Now that we have examined some of the many advantages of relaxation in daily life, let's look at a situation in which special benefit can be derived from relaxation - pregnancy and childbirth.

Calmness Despite the Changes

During pregnancy, the mother's body changes, adapting itself to the development of the fetus. Muscles tire more quickly and store up tension. Hormonal activity reaches a peak during pregnancy, affecting physical and emotional states. Therefore, daily practice of the *"12-Minute Pause"* is critical during this special period to relieve tension, adjust to the physical changes in the body, and be calm and relaxed, both, physically and emotionally.

Strengthening the Connection with the Fetus

Today it is known that the feelings and thoughts of the mother have a direct impact on the baby before it is born. The unborn baby absorbs the mother's thoughts and feels the emotions communicated to it (not always consciously). When the message conveyed is one of anxiety, fear, or lack of acceptance, this can adversely affect development during and after pregnancy. On the other hand, messages of love and acceptance make an enormous contribution to proper development.

In a state of relaxation, concerns, anxieties, fears, and negative thoughts disappear. It's easier to think positively in this state and to create a better connection with the fetus – to feel it, soothe it, speak to it rationally, and convey messages of love, acceptance, and warmth.

Preparation for Birth

Childbirth requires the muscles of the uterus to work hard. What do people do who have to prepare for heavy physical exertion - athletes, for example? Answer: They practice!

Similarly, if you have to undergo heavy exertion during childbirth, it's crucial that you practice beforehand. This preparation includes getting information about the upcoming experience, learning how to breathe correctly during the delivery, and learning relaxation.

Let's look at the connection between learning how to relax and preparing for childbirth. You'll be able to use relaxation techniques during the stages of dilation (opening). Relaxation will help you dissipate emotional stress and release muscle tension. Through relaxation, you will be calm, strong, and in control throughout.

When the contractions come more frequently, the body concentrates its energy in the effort to help the baby come out. The ability to relax the muscles after each contraction helps open up the birth canal; that is, it allows an easier childbirth. A woman who practices relaxation does not keep her muscles tight between contractions, and does not contract the cervix, thus easing the process of dilation.

It's important to practice relaxation prior to childbirth so that it will become automatic and can be used between contractions.

If the contractions occur very frequently, every five minutes or so, it would be good for your partner, if he is by your side, to "remind" you to relax your body after every contraction.

Your level of calmness and your attitude toward the pain are also significant factors. A nervous and fearful woman giving birth has a negative effect on the process of childbirth, both on herself and on the baby. In contrast, a calm woman will feel less pain and can focus better on the birth process.

Another advantage to relaxation is that it helps you control your thoughts and create an emotional connection with the baby. Don't forget that the baby is a human being with feelings and a memory. Speak to it, tell it "Mother loves you and is awaiting your arrival." In this way you can focus on the most important part – the arrival of your baby into the world – and feel the pain less.

To prepare for childbirth do the following exercise a few days before, to help program your mind for an easy and safe delivery:

Exercise for Childbirth

Close your eyes and relax your body from head to toe, as you did in the *"12-Minute Pause."* Envision yourself in your personal place and imagine that you're in the process of giving birth to your baby. You're located in the place you chose to give birth. You're there with your partner and the medical staff who will help with the delivery. You feel safe and calm. Now you feel a contraction. When the contraction is over, relax yourself even more. Let a wave of relaxation flow into you.

Remember that every contraction brings closer the arrival of your child into the world. Imagine that its head is already in the birth canal.

With every contraction, the baby descends and pushes a little more, and the cervix opens and widens, opens and widens. The delivery is proceeding in a natural manner. Now the contractions are stronger. A new feeling arises – a desire to push. Now you're fully open. You feel the baby pushing downward.

Help it come out. Push, push with each contraction. Breathe deeply and push. When the contraction ends, relax and gather strength for the next one. Again a contraction and the head appears. With the next contraction the baby comes out. Continue to push and the entire body is out.

You breathe easier, smile, and accept the baby into your arms to give it warmth and love.

Appendix A

The Loss of a Loved One

*These reflections are dedicated
to our good friend Rivka Cohen,
in memory of her son Nitzan,
who died at the age of 22.*

At a certain point in our life we must cope with the death of a loved one. When a young person dies we sense injustice, a disturbance of the natural order of things.

However, our presence in this world is not measured by the number of years that we spend on earth. The author Stephan Levine tells us that American Indians do not describe life the same way we do.

In our culture life is thought of in linear notions, a straight line that gets better as the length is increases. In contrast, in American Indian cultures a person's life is not considered a line but a circle. The importance is not how long a person lives, but how he lives every moment of his existence.

We can all choose either to continue lamenting the loss of a loved one, or to continue our lives in the best possible way. To accomplish the latter, we must remember the positive experiences that we shared, and the good times that we spent together with those who are no longer with us, and feel that all those moments still live on in us. Although the person is no longer physically with us, the feelings and positive memories still live in our hearts.

All the values that flourished in this relationship – love, friendship, understanding, support, continue to be a part of us. When we remember those happy moments, we honor the deceased and we keep alive in ourselves the memory of his or her life, and not the pain that the death caused us.

No one can take away that which our loved ones gave us and which lives within us. All of the special moments that emerged from that relationship enable us to go on.

We must be thankful to our loved ones for all they gave us while being alive, and feel happy that by doing so we make them part of our lives. This will provide us with the necessary resources to continue leading productive lives.

British psychologist and writer Ursula Markham, upon the loss of her husband, received a poem from a friend. She tells us that the poem, presented below, helped her overcome her agony:

Death is nothing at all. I have only slipped away into the next room.
I am I, and you are you. Whatever we were to each other, we are still.
Call me by my old familiar name.
Speak to me in the easy way which you always used to.
Put no difference into your tone.
Wear no forced air of solemnity or sorrow.
Laugh as we always laughed at the little jokes we enjoyed together.
Play... smile... think of me... pray for me.
Let my name be ever the household word that it always was.
Let it be spoken without effect, without a ghost of a shadow on it.
Life means all that it ever meant. It is the same as it ever was.
There is absolutely unbroken continuity.
What is this death, but a negligible accident?
Why should I be out of mind because I am out of sight?

I am but waiting for you... for an interval.
Somewhere very near – just around the corner
All is well.

We wish to thank Element Books for permission to quote this poem
from the book: "Bereavement" by Ursula Markham

Appendix B

And What Now?

Relaxation begins with a single, small step – sitting comfortably in a chair, eyes closed, and trying to relax each and every part of your body. That's the first step.

The more you do the *"12-Minute Pause,"* the more you'll be aware of yourself. You'll be able to relax your body, control the process, relieve tension, be in touch with your inner consciousness, and take advantage of inner resources to create positive changes in your life.

You'll feel better about yourself, more tolerant toward others, and more eager as you approach your day-to-day activities. You'll feel more open, both mentally and emotionally. You'll be able to sustain the calmness and openness that you acquired during relaxation throughout the day. You'll be able to use relaxation in every situation – in the office, standing in line, waiting at a red light, or just sitting and watching TV.

There's no need to close your eyes. Notice that the muscles in your shoulders and other parts of your body are not contracted unnecessarily. Notice your breathing. Try to breathe from your abdomen. This is how relaxation can become part of you. Doing the *"12-Minute Pause"* and carrying out the appropriate exercises from this book will reinforce this skill and it will become another positive step in your personal growth.

The Silva Method

This book is based on the Silva Method, and we hope that you have benefited from your reading and your practice of the techniques.

Since you may like to know more about this method, we are including a basic overview of the course.

The Silva Method is an international method developed by American researcher Jose Silva, born in Laredo, Texas in 1914. To this day, Silva continues to teach and lecture on the method all over the world.

Silva began his research in 1944 to help his ten children perform better at school. Later, he successfully trained a group of 39 children.

Silva's research led him to develop a method that would meet the needs of the public at large, a method that would train people to find solutions and to better cope with daily life.

In 1966, Jose Silva gave his first course to a group of art students. The method spread throughout the United States and then throughout the world. Today, centers teach the Silva Method in 104 countries around the globe. The Silva Method has been translated into 29 languages and millions of people derive benefit from it.

The course for learning the Silva Method includes lectures and of mental training exercises suitable for every age. It is a practical course, with training in all the techniques. It is not group therapy nor are personal problems discussed. The pleasant atmosphere and positive attitude of the course foster a calm, relaxed feeling. The background of the participants – educational and personal – is irrelevant. Through this course, people from every walk of life can significantly improve the quality of their lives.

The first level of the Silva Method is conveyed in the basic course through four stages: Controlled Relaxation, Personal Growth, Development of Intuition and Creativity, and Practical Applications.

Controlled Relaxation

The first stage of the course teaches relaxation. You have already learned the basics; during the course you can improve your skills within the context of the group and attain deeper levels of relaxation through a series of exercises.

Relaxation is the basis of all the techniques learned throughout the course. In this first stage, you learn how to use the state of relaxation to think positively, by controlling your imagination.

Afterwards, you learn techniques that enable you to overcome insomnia, to awaken on time without an alarm clock, to stay awake when necessary, to relieve headaches and migraines, and also to use dreams for information needed to solve problems. You learn to remember your dreams and to draw solutions out of them that do not otherwise emerge. This is possible because the dream connects the conscious mind with the inner consciousness. You can use the mind to sleep better, to overcome nightmares, and to "program" pleasant dreams.

Personal Growth

At this stage of the course, you learn what the mind is capable of doing on your behalf and how to use it. Our mental abilities are enormous, but in common functioning, the mind is beset by a large number of stimuli that appear simultaneously and at high frequency: thoughts, desires, needs, noises, pressures, etc. It's hard to focus full attention on any one thing unless you're in a state of relaxation.

But most people are in this state only prior to falling asleep and don't know how to take advantage of it. People don't generally know that it's possible to achieve relaxation or how to use it for their benefit.

Through techniques applied during a state of relaxation, the Silva Method lets you discover talents within yourself and to express them in the desired areas.

You learn to create a "mental screen" for developing the imagination and to use "code words" to improve concentration and memory. You acquire the "Three Fingers Technique" for fast and easy learning, for remembering written material and lectures, and for improving your performance on exams. You also learn to overcome unwanted habits and physical pain (through the techniques of "Hand Levitation" and "Glove Anesthesia").

Later, you use a technique called "The Mirror of the Mind" to attain objectives in business, work, interpersonal relations, family relationships, and others. You also learn the techniques of choosing among various options (the "Glass of Water" technique) to help you make the best decision.

Development of Intuition and Creativity

Everyone has intuition. How many times has it happened to you that the phone rang and you knew who was calling? Or you had a strong feeling that something would happen and it did? Or you had a dream that came true a short while later? Through intuition, you can obtain important information, for example, about future business trends, good (and bad) investments, or whether or not to embark upon a particular business.

You can use intuition to better understand people you meet or have to deal with – their motivations, feelings, or needs, and how to create better relationships with them.

Intuition helps solve problems that seem irresolvable, and helps you make better decisions, because you have more information.

Often, people do not rely on their intuition. Has it ever happened that you did not rely on your intuition, and later regretted it?

People who are more open, with a better-developed intuition, accept information in a spontaneous and unbiased manner. In the Silva Method course you learn how to develop and sharpen your intuition through a series of exercises and experiments (with metals, plants, and animals). These experiments enable us to use our imagination to receive information beyond sensory data, in order to utilize all the options available to us to solve problems, score accomplishments, and achieve goals.

The "Mental Laboratory" technique supplies the framework that directs the brain to discover creative ideas. The "counselors" you create in the Mental Laboratory are another way to reinforce your creative ability. Through imagination, you will create new points of reference in order to expand the receptivity of your physical senses.

A point of reference is something familiar that enables us to take in new information. To explain what we mean by points of reference, Burt Goldman uses this analogy:

"Let's say that a caveman, someone who lived 50,000 years ago, is brought into the center of a busy city in the present era. It's quite possible that his mental circuits would become so overloaded with impressions that the system would simply shut down to additional stimuli.

"So let's take him far away from there and place him in the middle of the desert, a place that might remind him of an environment he could have encountered in the earlier era. And now, let's show him a shiny red car. What would be his reaction? Would he think of it as an automobile? As some form of transportation?

"Not in a million years! The caveman has absolutely no reference point that he can use to relate to the car. He has never seen anything so bizarre. Chances are he would see little more than a rock. A wet rock, because it's shiny. He knows that wet rocks are shinier than dry ones.

"If one of us were to open the door of the car and get in, his mouth would probably drop open in astonishment: A hollow rock! A hollow rock means a cave – a really peculiar looking cave.

However, if we were to start the car, it's anybody's guess what his reaction to that would be. He might panic; he might faint; it might be too much for him. Rocks may do strange things now and then, but to suddenly emit all that racket, and then buzz off into the distance would be far beyond the reference point of the caveman. So let's make it easier for him by building the car in stages.

"First we take a tree trunk and cut four slices off it. A log is nothing new, so he looks upon this one without particular reaction. When he picks up one of the cutoff sections, he may wonder about its shape, but wood is still familiar enough not to throw him. But, as for seeing a potential wheel in that slab in his hand, no; wheels have yet to be invented, so it's still completely outside his frame of reference.

"Our next step is to knock holes in the middle of the four round tree-trunk sections. Then we find two suitably straight branches as axles and mount a pair of round sections on each. The potential utility of this contraption still escapes the caveman.

"Now we'll do something interesting. We'll place the two axles and their wheels a short distance apart, and start laying straight branches across them, fastening them together with strips of leather. Little by little, it forms the bed of a very crude vehicle.

"Aha! Now perhaps at this point the first faint glimmering might appear in the mind of our caveman. All the materials are familiar to him – pieces of log, branches, and sticks – but in a new, totally different configuration that he has never seen before.

"Then we push it and it rolls. We coax him onto the thing, and he takes a short ride. More understanding dawns. At the next stage we get some more branches and form a body for the car; we cover it with skins, leaving openings for the "windows." Finally we put the cart of sticks and skins alongside the actual car and watch our caveman compare them. Only now, as the points of reference were developed for him one by one, can he grasp the idea of the car being some sort of vehicle.

This same process takes place during the course. Part after part, step by step, you develop points of reference that enable you to understand, internalize, and benefit from the advanced material at the end of the course."

Practical Applications

At this final stage of the course, you apply what was learned in the previous stages and create new reference points for using the imagination to solve problems and to help yourself and others.

Each participant learns to envision the human anatomy from a spiritual point of view, to absorb how he or she functions when everything is in proper working order. At the end of the course, everyone participates in a final exercise and discovers skills that he or she had not realized existed to describe information through the imagination for solving problems and helping others.

Development of these skills helps enhance personal success on both the material and spiritual levels.

In addition to the basic course described above, the Silva Institute offers advanced courses, applied workshops, and seminars that deepen and expand on special subjects dealt with by the Method.

The Silva Method is not just for adults. Jose Silva also developed a special course for children between the ages of 7 and 13. Children learn the method easily and quickly because their brain is still open and flexible, able to absorb principles of self-control and positive thinking. This approach will help them cope with difficulties in life and enjoy better health.

Children in the course acquire tools that help them control unwanted habits, overcome their fears, sleep well at night, and awaken in the morning without an alarm clock.

The children learn how to improve their concentration and sharpen their memory to help them in their studies. They learn how to study and to prepare for exams more easily.

Children learn to create good relationships with others parents, brothers and sisters, friends, and teachers. The course gives them the tools to solve problems efficiently and well, to set goals for themselves, and to carry out the suitable programming for turning a goal into reality. The techniques of the course will hold them in good stead throughout their lives, and will increase their chances of growing up to be happy adults.

Apendix C

Study

THE SILVA METHOD AND ANXIETY LEVEL

Rafael Liberman

The Silva Method is a system for training the mind based on relaxation combined with the development of visualization, imagination and intuition. This article examines the effects of the method on individual anxiety levels immediately upon completion of the course and after a time interval has passed. Variables such as age, gender, frequency of exercise and profession have also been studied. The results validate the hypothesis that after taking the Silva Method course, an individual's level of anxiety is significantly lower than the starting level. Variances in frequency of practice, gender and age were also shown to affect the level of anxiety among course graduates.

Foreword

Holistic medicine is concerned with the whole individual in his environment, and concentrates on the prevention or cure of illness. Health is defined as "a state of physical, mental and spiritual well-being, in harmony with the natural and social environments, and not as the absence of sickness." (1) The "General Adaptation Syndrome"

The article presented here is a summary of a study carried out through the Psychology Department of the University of Haifa, under the supervision of Dr. Moshe Almagor. The author wishes to thank Dr. Carlos Feizer (University of Haifa) and Zippi Liberman (University of Tel Aviv) for their valuable comments. The author would also like to thank "The Silva Method Institute in Israel" and the course graduates who participated in the study.

theory (2) suggests that all life experiences are tension-producing, but that the healthy body is capable of adapting to them. Non-adaptation to stress may cause illness, which can attack the weakest part of the organism. Selye (2) asserts that there is not only a direct relationship between stress and illness, but also that a high level of stress accelerates the aging process. These symptoms can be overcome through relaxation, because relaxation constitutes the physiological factor opposite to tension and anxiety.

Certain methods, such as Transcendental Meditation (4), Zen meditation (5), and progressive relaxation (6) succeed in reducing the general level of stress and anxiety. Other methods, such as Autogenics Training (7), Systematic Desensitization (3), and Mind Control (8) enhance utilization of controlled imagination in the relaxed state, as the principal tension-reducing instrument. Jaffe and Bresler (9) demonstrate that controlled imagination can have therapeutic effects.

The Silva Method, which accepts holistic principles, is a method of relaxation and controlled imagination; it provides directed techniques not only for the reduction of stress, but also for the improvement of health and problem-solving. The method teaches how to consciously utilize the mind to accomplish proposed goals with the aid of suitable programming. In the Silva method, "to program," means to direct one's mental energies towards the proposed goal (10).

The specific aim of the Silva method is to teach the subject to think while in a state of relaxation, and while in this state, to utilize proper programming techniques to accomplish fixed goals.

Whereas in techniques such as yoga and Transcendental Meditation the subject reaches passive relaxation, with the Silva Method he or she achieves 'active' relaxation. The methods also differ in the practical nature of the techniques and in the capacity to utilize them to solve specific problems and develop a strategy for the solution of future problems.

The Silva Method is not hypnosis, because the subject remains conscious and completely in control while practicing the techniques; he remains mentally active during the exercise and is not dependent on any external agent.

As opposed to biofeedback (11), the Silva Method provides techniques for solving specific problems without the use of any apparatus.

Silva (8) asserts that his methods encompass techniques of dynamic meditation, which teach the individual to activate the mind while in a relaxed state, utilizing inner resources for solving problems.

Various investigations have demonstrated the influence of the method on personality variables (10, 12, 13).

De Sau and Seawell (12) measured the changes produced in personality variables of men and women who participated in one of the courses, both before and after training. The participants achieved significant changes in their ego force, self-confidence, initiative, and capacity for relaxation. A post-course investigation concerning the changes produced in different personality variables was conducted with secondary school pupils (13). The subjects came from three high schools in the United States: "Hallahan" for women, "Lawrenceville" (coeducational), and "St. Fidelis" for men.

Measurements were made immediately following the course in all these schools, and four and five months later at the "Lawrenceville" and "St. Fidelis" schools, respectively. There were significant changes in many personality variables (13) measured by the "High School Personality Questionnaire." (3)

Tamayo (10) concluded that, "The Silva Method significantly influenced the reduction of neuroticism, decreased introversion, strengthened coping ability and the ego, neutralized the tendency towards guilt feelings, provided release from stress and frustration, and led to the founding of improved social orientation."

One study was conducted within the framework of the Institute for Social Services in Michigan (14) on the effect of the method on the self-image of unemployed mothers. The mothers who volunteered for the study were randomly divided into an experimental group (whose members took the course for mind control) and a control group. A significant improvement in self image was found in the mothers in the experimental group, as measured on the TENNESEE SELF CONCEPT SCALE (TSCS), and no significant improvement in self-image was found in the control group. The researchers examined the effect of the method on personality change and self-image. There has been no previous study that specifically studies the effect of the method on the level of trait anxiety, and this is the objective of the present study.

Anxiety is "a reaction of the individual to a situation perceived as threatening to him" (15). Anxiety can be aroused by external stimuli which threaten the ego, or by internal stimuli, that cause the individual to anticipate danger (15). In light of the work done by Cattell and Schier (16), Spielberger (17) developed the theory of 'trait anxiety' and 'state anxiety.' The theory asserts that anxiety is a two-dimensional emotion. One dimension is *state anxiety,* which is a passing, unpleasant emotional experience characterized by tension, worry, suspicion and discomfort. The second dimension, *trait anxiety,* reflects interpersonal differences in a person's potential to experience situation anxiety and his capacity to respond to situations that are perceived to be threatening. Persons with a high level of trait anxiety are more susceptible than others to identifying threatening stimuli, and they experience more frequent and more powerful situation anxiety. Individuals with a high level of trait anxiety may also tend to respond with maladaptive behavior, such as exaggerated concern about themselves or the situation. In some instances, they may be unable to cope with the pressure in a coherent manner (18).

If the Silva Method can reduce the level of *trait anxiety* in an individual, it will have a positive effect in reinforcing adaptive behavior. This report will investigate whether or not the Silva method can reduce a person's level of trait anxiety either in the short term or in the long term. Effects of variables such as age, gender, occupation, and frequency of practice of the techniques will be taken into consideration.

METHODOLOGY

Subjects: 374 individuals who took the Silva Method course in Israel (115 men and 259 women), ranging in age from 16 to 70 (men: M = 37.6, women: M = 38.15) and active in a wide range of occupations.

Tools: For adults, the Spielberger Questionnaire (1972) was used as it appears in Taichman and Melinak's Hebrew version of the "State-Trait Anxiety Inventory" (25), a self-descriptive questionnaire consisting of 40 items, 20 of which refer to state anxiety and 20 of which refer to trait anxiety.

In the state anxiety questionnaire, the subject is asked how he feels at a particular moment, describing emotions characteristic of anxiety (tension, preoccupation, and nervousness), as well as emotions in which anxiety is absent (relaxation, tranquility, security). The subject indicates his feelings at a given moment, according to the following scale: "hardly ever," "sometimes," "often," and "almost always."

The trait anxiety questionnaire is more general. The subject is asked to describe his feelings in general.

The present investigation used only the trait anxiety questionnaire, with the objective of studying the possible effect of the method on a personality variable such as trait anxiety. In order to measure the effect of technique application, subjects were asked how often they practice (once, twice, or three times a day, or not at all.) The subjects were divided into two groups: those who practice (those who responded that they practice at least once a day) and those who do not (those who indicated that they do not practice, or who stated they practice on an average of less than once a day).

To 'practice' means to perform a relaxation exercise which utilizes Silva Method techniques studied in the course for a 5 - 15 minute period, from one to three times a day.

HYPOTHESES

1. The level of trait anxiety immediately after the course will be significantly lower than the level of trait anxiety at the beginning of the course.

2. The level of trait anxiety six months (average) after the start of the course will be significantly lower than the level of trait anxiety at the beginning of the course.

3. Immediately after the course the level of trait anxiety of those subjects who practice at least once a day will be significantly lower than the level of trait anxiety of those subjects who do not practice, who practice on an average of less than once a day.

4. Six months (average) after the beginning of the course the level of trait anxiety of those subjects who practice at least once a day will be significantly lower than the level of trait anxiety of those subjects who do not practice, or who practice on an average of less than once a day.

PROCEDURE

First Stage: Pre-test

Participants filled out the trait anxiety questionnaire on the first day of the course, immediately following the first break and before the actual presentation of the Silva Method techniques. Participants taking the course for the second time specified this on the questionnaire. In some cases, these were used as a third measurement.

At this stage, the subjects' trait anxiety level at the outset of the course was measured.

Second Stage: Post-test

On the final day of the course, following the last break, the subjects again filled out the questionnaire. The subjects' trait anxiety level on completion of the course was measured, and information was obtained concerning their frequency of practice.

Third Stage: Follow-up

The third measurement was taken at the graduate's meetings. After the first break, the questionnaire was again distributed to the subjects. In the case of a large amount of data for the same person, the most recent data were considered. At this stage, trait anxiety was measured on an average of 25 weeks (SD = 16.28) after the beginning of the course, and information as to frequency of practice was noted for this period. Efforts were made to locate those graduates who did not appear at the graduates meeting so that there would be a third measurement for these people as well. A questionnaire was sent by mail to those who did not come to the reunion, along with a letter asking them to fill out the data and return it as soon as possible. Those who did not participate in the reunions received the questionnaire by mail, along with a letter asking them to fill it out and return it as soon as possible. Those who failed to return the questionnaire within a reasonable period of time were telephoned and asked to do so. In some instances, questionnaires were again sent out. Ninety-four questionnaires were thereby received.

The Results

Graph 1: Level of trait anxiety of graduates of the Silva Method training course at varied measurements according to gender.

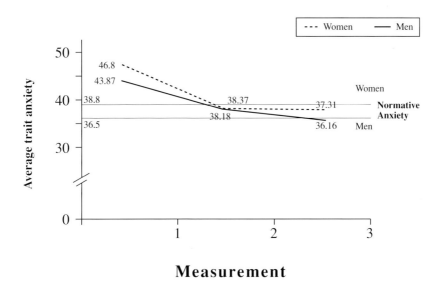

Measurement

Graph 1 shows the changes in levels of average trait anxiety which occurred in Silva Method training course graduates under varied measurements for both sexes. The significant difference between the sexes was found in their beginning levels of anxiety (men: M = 43.87, women: M = 46.80 ; t = 2.49, p<0.01). For this reason it was decided that the continuation of the study would take into consideration the gender of the individuals and analyze the results separately for men and for women.

TABLE 1: Average improvement, according to sex, in trait anxiety level of Silva Method graduates in the post-test and follow-up stages.

Improvement Sample		Post test	t	Follow- up	t
Women	M	8.43	18.04*	9.78	15.96*
	Sd	7.52		8.44	
Men	M	5.69	9.37*	7.54	7.74*
	Sd	6.51		8.08	

* p<0.001

The results shown in Table 1 support the first hypothesis, which asserts that the average level of trait anxiety of subjects of both sexes, immediately after the course, will be significantly lower than their average level at the beginning of the course.

These results also support the second hypothesis(*), which asserts that the average level of trait anxiety an average of six months after the course will be significantly lower than the trait anxiety level at the beginning of the course.

In the variation analysis, no significant difference was found in the trait anxiety improvement of individuals of different professions ($F (11,362 = 1.25$) immediately after the course. Also, a significant negative correlation (the younger the individual, the greater the improvement) was found between age and improvement in trait anxiety for women in the post test stage ($r = -0.23$; p 0.0001) and in the follow-up stage ($r = -0.25$; p<0.001), and for men in the post-test stage ($r = -0.23$; p 0.01).

(*) Note 1: The second and fourth hypotheses were confirmed for 69% of the total sample.

Graph 2: Effect of practice on the improvement of trait anxiety immediately after the course and follow-up, by gender.

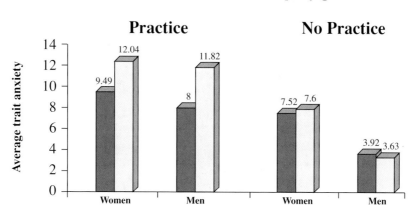

In Graph 2 it is possible to see the positive effect of practice on the level of trait anxiety immediately after the course and after six months from the start of the course for both sexes. No significant difference was found in the initial level of trait anxiety between those who practiced and those who did not.

The results of the variation analysis support the third hypothesis; they demonstrate that there is a significant difference, at the post-test stage, in improvement in trait anxiety level (F (1,303) = 9.89; p<0.01) among those who practice (at least once a day). The data show that practice has a strong influence on trait anxiety level improvement over a period of time (F = (3,251) = 30.24; p<0.0001). The results thus reinforce the fourth hypothesis (see Note 1 on previous page).

As shown in Table 1, the average level of trait anxiety of participants in the Silva Method course is significantly higher than the normative level of trait anxiety (p<0.0001).

In the post-test stage, for both sexes, no significant differences were observed between trait anxiety of course graduates and the normative level of trait anxiety, except that the men had a significantly higher trait anxiety level ($p<0.0001$) than that of the soldiers in the normative sample.

In the follow-up stage, the women's trait anxiety level was significantly lower than various normative samples: soldiers ($p<0.01$); students ($p<0.0001$); adolescents ($p<0.01$). The trait anxiety level of the men investigated was not significantly different from that of the normative sample for soldiers ($p<0.05$).

DISCUSSION

The present report investigated the influence of the Silva Method on the subjects' trait anxiety level, both upon completion of the course and at long term.

The first hypothesis asserted that the trait anxiety level of the subjects, upon completion of the course, would be significantly lower than at the beginning of the course; the second hypothesis asserted that the change would continue with time. The results support both hypotheses.

The third hypothesis asserted that upon completion of the course, the trait anxiety level of individuals who practice would be significantly lower than that of individuals who did not practice; the fourth hypothesis asserted that this difference would continue to exist with the passing of time. Both hypotheses were confirmed.

The difference in the degree of improvement in those subjects who practiced, as opposed to those who did not practice, was accentuated over a period of time F (1,303) = 9.89, p<0.01 in the post-test stage, as opposed to F(3,251) = 30.24, p<0.0001 in the follow-up stage.

A probable explanation is that every participant practices during the course and therefore, those subjects catalogued as non-practicing did practice at least twice a week (during the course), while some of them practiced even more, albeit irregularly (on the average of less than once a day). This explains why the difference between those subjects who practiced and those who did not, upon completion of the course, is significant, but less so than the difference between these groups over time. These findings illustrate the importance of daily practice in reducing the level of trait anxiety, although the trait anxiety level of those who did not practice daily, also improved considerably (p<0.0001).

It is probable that the subjects who practiced and those who did not, differ not only in the reduction of the trait anxiety level after the course, but also in other personality variables which were not checked in the present investigation.

A certain tendency was found towards a gender-related differential effect of practice: men who did not practice improved less than women who did not practice, both upon completion of the course and over the long term. A possible explanation for this finding may lie in the personality difference between the sexes. Some investigators assert that the level of Factor A (affectothymia) and factor I (premsia) in women, is greater than that in men (19). Therefore, women tend to be more open to people, less critical, and more sensitive.

Weitzenhoffer (20), found that women have higher hypnotic suggestibility than men. These characteristics may explain why the effect of the techniques learned in the course are stronger on women than on men. It is possible that women are more open and sensitive to the material learned in the course, and therefore the practice during the course and infrequent practice afterwards were sufficient for the women to reduce their level of trait anxiety more than men who practiced an equivalent amount. It is important to note that a significant difference was found in the level of beginning anxiety between those who practiced and those who did not and thus the differences in the amount of improvement came about due to the influence of the ceiling effect.*

The researchers saw a connection between the positive approach of women and their suggestibility (21,22) and it may be that the approach of women to the course is on the whole, more positive than that of men. However, this is only a hypothesis which would need to be examined. As to the age factor, it was found that the younger the participant in the course, the more improvement in reduction of anxiety immediately following the course. Six months after the course (on the average) from the start of the course, the correlation with age was a factor only among women. As mentioned above, persons who take the Silva Method course exhibit an average level of trait anxiety which is higher than the average.

On the basis of this finding, it is possible to assume that one of the motivating factors for course participation is the relatively high level of anxiety of the participants to begin with.
Immediately after the course was concluded, the participants succeeded in attaining a normative anxiety level (excluding the soldier sample whose level of trait anxiety was significantly lower $p < 0.001$ than the men in the study).

---

* ceiling effect: Those subjects with a hight trait anxiety have more range to improve than those whose trait anxiety is lower.

An average of six months after the beginning of the course, women participants attained a level of trait anxiety significantly lower than normative, while men reached the normative level (except for the soldiers, whose level was considerably lower: $p<0.05$).

As can be observed, the improvement of women is greater than that of men; this could be a consequence of the "ceiling effect." The results contradict Spielberger's theory (15, 17), which asserts that relatively short-term methods will not reduce the level of trait anxiety, but only the level of state anxiety. The results of the present investigation are supported by other studies, which have shown that graduates of the course improved their self-confidence, self-image, and other personality variables (10, 12, 13, 14), which might possibly be related to the reduction of the trait anxiety level. There are various possible explanations for the graduates' improvement in trait anxiety level, despite the relative brevity of the course (twice a week for five weeks or two weekends):

1. The course provides a more positive attitude towards life experiences, and emphasizes the importance of positive thinking.
2. The course provides specific programming techniques wich can be utilized by the individual as a means to solve daily problems
3. The course is practical, and encompasses exercise of all the techniques.
4. The pleasant atmosphere during the course, as well as the positive attitude of the course leaders, contribute to relaxation and tranquility.

In addition, the results obtained tend to contradict the assertion that only long-term therapy can reduce the level of trait anxiety of the individual. However, they have not yet shown that the improvement attained is due solely to the techniques learned in the course. One of the limitations of this investigation is that the third measurement was made on those subjects who participated in one of the graduate's meetings or who sent the questionnaire in by mail. Moreover, because of the lack of a control group, it cannot be shown that the reduction of the level of trait anxiety is due solely to the influence of the course. Stoudenmire (23) was unable to show significant influence of muscular relaxation on the level of trait anxiety of introverts and extroverts. In another investigation (24), it was found that the level of trait anxiety of individuals is not significantly affected by muscular relaxation through music. Therefore, it should not be assumed that the reduction in the trait anxiety of course graduates is due exclusively to the relaxation techniques learned during the course. In accordance with the results obtained, however, the Silva Method course does appear to provide an efficient means for reduction of the level of trait anxiety. There are indications that, in spite of the influence of modifying variables, the method exerts a significant influence on trait anxiety.

BIBLIOGRAPHY

1. Mattson P.H. *"Holistic Health in Perspective"* USA: Mayfield Publishing Corporation, 1982.

2. Selye H. *"Stress Without Distress"* Philadelphia & New York: Lippincott, 1974.

3. Wolpe J. *"Psychotherapy by Reciprocal Inhibition,"* California: Stanford University Press, 1958.

4. Wallace R.K. *"Physiological Effects of TM"* Science 167 1751-54, 1970.

5. Kasamatsu & Hirai. *"An Electroencephalografic Study of the Zen Meditation (Zasen),"*In Targ. C. *"Alterated States of Conciousness,"* New York: Willey, 1969, 489-501.

6. Jacobson E. *"Progressive Relaxation."*Chicago: University of Chicago Press, 1938.

7. Brown B. "Supermind, the Ultimate Energy." New York: Harper & Row, 1980.

8. Silva J. & Miele P. *"The Silva Mind Control Method."* New York: Simon & Schuster, 1977.

9. Jaffe & Bresler D.E. *"Guided Imagery Healing Through the Mind's Eye."* In Gordon J.S., Jaffe D.T. & Bresler D.E *"Mind, Body,and Health,"* New York: Human Sciences Press, 1984.

10. *Tamayo U.P."Control Mental y Personalidad."* Study presented at Complutense University of Madrid, Mexico: Offset Multicolor, 1981.

11. Brown B. "Stress and the Art of Biofeedback." New York: Harper & Row, 1977.

12. De Sau G.T. & Seawell, *"The Albuquerque Report."* Laredo Texas: SMCI, 1974.

13. De Sau G.T. *"The Silva Mind Control Course Effects with Three High School Populations."* Laredo Texas: SMCI, 1974.

14. Mottiff J. As appeared in Wallace D.A. *"The Ottawa County Project."* Laredo, Texas: SMCI, 1974

15. Spielberger C.D. *"The Nature and Measurement of Anxiety."* In Spielberger C.D. & Guerrero D. *"Cross-Cultural Research on Anxiety."* Washington D.C.: Hemisphere Publishing Corporation, Willey, 1976.

16. Catell R.B. & Schier I.H. *"The Meaning and Measurement of Neuroticism and Anxiety."* New York: Willey, 1963.

17. Spielberger C.D. *"Anxiety and Behavior."* USA: 1966.

18. Houston K.B. *"Trait Anxiety & Cognitive Coping Behavior."* In Krohne W. & Laux L. *"Achievement, Stress, and Anxiety."* USA: Hemisphere Publishing Corporation 1982, Ch. 9, 195-206.

19. Buss A.R. & Poley W. *"Individual Differences Traits and Factors."* New York: Gardner Press, Inc., 1976.

20. Weitzenhoffer A.M. *"Hypnotism: An Objective Study in Suggestibility."* New York: Willey, 1953.

21. Rosehand D. & Tomkins S.S. *"On Preference for Hypnosis and Hypnotizability."* Int. J. Clin. Exp. Hyp. 12 109-14, 1964.

22. Hilgard E.R. *"Hypnotic Suggestibility."* New York: Harcourt, Brace & Javanovich, 1965.

23. Stoudenmire J. *"Effects of Muscle Relaxation Training on State and Trait Anxiety in Introverts and Extroverts."* J. Pers. & Social Psychol. 24 (2)273-5, No. 72.

24. *"A Comparison of Muscle Relaxation Training and Music in the Reduction of State and Trait Anxiety".* J. Clin. Psychol. 31(3) 490-2, Jl. 75

25. Taichman A. & Melniak I. *"Manual for the State Trait Anxiety Inventory"* Ramot: Tel Aviv University Press, Second Edition, 1984 (In Hebrew)

Recommended Reading List

Achterberg J. *Imagery in Healing*. Shambala, Boston: 1985.

Benson H. *The Relaxation Response*. Avon, New York: 1975.

Benson H. *The Mind-Body Effect*. Simon & Schuster, New York: 1979.

Benson H. & Stark M. *Timeless Healing The Power & Biology of Belief*. Scribner, New York: 1996

Bloch D. & Merrit J. *El Pensamiento Positivo y los Niño*s. Los Libros del Comienzo, Madrid: 1995.

Brown B. *Stress and the Art of Biofeedback*. Harper & Row, New York: 1977.

Brown B. Supermind *Ultimate Energy*. Bantam Books, New York: 1983.

Chopra D. *Quantum Healing Exploring the Frontiers of Mind/Body Medicine*. Bantam Books, New York: 1989.

Chopra D. *Ageless Body, Timeless Mind*. Harmony Books, New York: 1993.

Coxhead N. *Mindpower*. Unwin Paperbacks, London: 1987.

Diamond J. *Kinesiología del Comportamiento*. Edaf S.A., Madrid: 1980.

De Sau G.T. *The Silva Mind Control Course Effects With Three High School Populations*. SMCI, Laredo, Texas: 1974.

De Sau G.T. & Seawell *The Albequerque Report*. SMCI, Laredo, Texas: 1974.

Dossey L. *Healing Words The Power of Prayer & the Practice of Medicine*. HarperCollins Publishers, Inc., New York: 1993

Dyer W. You'll *See It When You Believe It*. William Morrow & Co., Inc., New York: 1989.

Dyer W. *Real Magic*. HarperCollins Publishers, Inc., New York: 1992.

Dyer W. *Your Sacred Self Making the Decision to be Free*. HarperCollins Publishers, Inc., New York: 1995.

Everly G. & Rosenfeld R. *The Nature and Treatment of the Stress Response*. Plenum Press, New York: 1981.

Everly G. & Sobelman S.A. *The Assessment of Human Response Neurological, Biochemical and Psychological Foundations*. AMS Press, New York: 1987.

Fanning P. *Visualization for Change*. New Harbiner Publications, Inc., Oakland: 1988.

Hay L. *You Can Heal Your life*. Hay House, Inc., California: 1984.

Hay L. *The Power is Within You*. Hay House, Inc., California: 1991.

Hay L. *Life!Reflexions on your Journey.* Hay House, Inc., California: 1995.

Hill N. *Think and Grow Rich.* Hawthorne Books, New York: 1967.

Hill N. & Stone C. *Success Through a Positive Mental Attitude.* Simon & Schuster, New York: 1977.

Holden-Lund C. *Effects of Relaxation with Guided Imagery on Surgical Stress and Wound Healing.* Research in Nursing & Health, 1988, 11. 235-244.

Jaffe D.T. *Healing From Within.* Simon & Schuster, New York: 1980.

Lazarus R. S. & Folkman S. *Stress Appraisal and Coping.* Springer Publishing Co., New York: 1984.

Lightsey O.R. *Thinking Positive as a Stress Buffer: The Role of Positive Automatic Cognitions in Depression and Happiness.* Journal of Counseling Psychology, 1994, 41, 325-334.

Locke S. & Colligan D. *The Healer Within.* Dutton, New York: 1986.

Murphy J. *The Power of Your Subconscious Mind.* Prentice Hall Inc., New York: 1963.

Nielsen G. & Polansky J. *Pendulum Power.* Inner Traditions, Vermont, New York: 1980.

Ornstein R. & Sobel D. *The Healing Brain.* Simon & Schuster, New York: 1987.

Peiffer V. *Positive Thinking*. Element Books Limited, Dorset: 1989.

Pelletier K. R. *Mind as Healer*, Mind as Slayer. Delacorte, New York: 1977.

Samuels M. & Samuels N. *Seeing with the Mind's Eye*. Random House, New York: 1975.

Siegel B.S. Love, *Medicine & Miracles*. Random House, New York: 1986.

Silva J. & Bernd E. Sales Power: *The Silva Mind Method for Sales Professionals*. Perigee Book, New York: 1982.

Silva J. & Bernd E. *The Silva Method Think and Grow Fit*. Career Press, New York: 1996.

Silva J. & Goldman B. *The Silva Mind Control Method of Mental Dynamics*. Simon & Schuster, New York: 1988.

Silva J. & Miele P. *The Silva Mind Control Method*. Simon & Schuster, New York: 1977.

Silva J. & Stone R. *You The Healer*. Kramer H.J., Inc., CA: 1989.

Silva J. & Stone R. *The Silva Mind Control Method for Getting Help from Your Other Side*. Simon & Schuster, New York: 1989.

Silva J. & Stone R. *The Silva Mind Control Method for Business Managers*. Prentice Hall Inc., New York: 1983.

Simonton S. *The Healing Family*. Bantam Books, New York: 1989.

Simonton C., Simonton S. & Creighton J. *Getting Well Again.* Bantam Books, New York: 1980.

Schafer W. *Stress Managment for Wellness.* Harcourt Brace Javanovich, Texas: 1992.

Smith J.C. *Understanding Stress and Coping.* Macmillan Pub Co. Inc, New York: 1993.

Verrier R.L. & Lown B. *Behavioral Stress and Cardiac Arrhythmias.* Annual Review of Physiology, 1984, 46, 155-176.

Weil A. *Natural Health, Natural Medicine.* Houghton Mifflin Co., New York: 1995.

Weil A. *Spontaneous Healing.* Ballantine Books, New York: 1996.

Weil A. *8 Weeks to Optimum Health.* Little, Brown & Co., London: 1997.

For further information about The Silva Method course please visit the Silva International web page at:

http//www.silvamethod.com
E-Mail: silva@Silvaintl.com